PRISM

LISTENING AND SPEAKING 2

Sabina Ostrowska
Nancy Jordan

with
Angela Blackwell
Janet Gokay

CAMBRIDGE
UNIVERSITY PRESS

CAMBRIDGE
UNIVERSITY PRESS

University Printing House, Cambridge CB2 8BS, United Kingdom

One Liberty Plaza, 20th Floor, New York, NY 10006, USA

477 Williamstown Road, Port Melbourne, VIC 3207, Australia

314–321, 3rd Floor, Plot 3, Splendor Forum, Jasola District Centre, New Delhi – 110025, India

79 Anson Road, #06–04/06, Singapore 079906

Cambridge University Press is part of the University of Cambridge.

It furthers the University's mission by disseminating knowledge in the pursuit of education, learning and research at the highest international levels of excellence.

www.cambridge.org
Information on this title: www.cambridge.org/9781316620977

First published 2017
20 19 18 17 16 15 14 13 12 11 10 9 8 7 6

Printed in Great Britain by CPI Group (UK) Ltd., Croydon CRO 4YY

A catalogue record for this publication is available from the British Library

ISBN 978-1-316-62097-7 Student's Book with Online Workbook 2 Listening and Speaking
ISBN 978-1-316-62516-3 Teacher's Manual 2 Listening and Speaking

CONTENTS

UNIT	WATCH AND LISTEN	LISTENINGS	LISTENING SKILLS	PRONUNCIATION FOR LISTENING	
1 ANIMALS *Academic Disciplines* Biology / Environmental Science / Zoology	The Mental Skills of Chimpanzees	1: A debate about using animals for work 2: A presentation about the human threats to polar bears	*Key Skills* Taking notes Listening for contrasting ideas Listening for signposting language *Additional Skills* Understanding key vocabulary Using your knowledge Listening for main ideas Listening for opinions Listening for text organization Listening for details Synthesizing	Intonation of lists	
2 THE ENVIRONMENT *Academic Disciplines* Ecology / Environmental Science / Political Science	Blowing in the Wind: Off-Shore Wind Farms	1: A lecture about agriculture 2: A debate about nuclear power	*Key Skills* Listening for explanations Listening for counterarguments *Additional Skills* Understanding key vocabulary Predicting content using visuals Listening for main ideas Listening for details Listening for text organization Taking notes Synthesizing	Connected speech: linking sounds	
3 TRANSPORTATION *Academic Disciplines* Civil Engineering / Psychology / Sociology	The Air Travel Revolution	1: A radio program about the fear of flying 2: A presentation about biking to work	*Key Skill* Listening for rhetorical questions *Additional Skills* Understanding key vocabulary Using your knowledge Listening for main ideas Listening for details Listening for text organization Taking notes Synthesizing	Word stress	
4 CUSTOMS AND TRADITIONS *Academic Disciplines* Anthropology / Cultural Studies / Sociology	The Chilean Cueca Brava	1: A radio program about changing customs in the modern world 2: A discussion about gift giving customs	*Key Skills* Identifying cause and effect Listening for opinion *Additional Skills* Understanding key vocabulary Using your knowledge Listening for main ideas Listening for details Taking notes Synthesizing	Connected speech: final /t/ and /d/	

LANGUAGE DEVELOPMENT	CRITICAL THINKING	SPEAKING	ON CAMPUS
Word families Modals for necessity and advice	Organizing information for a presentation	*Speaking Skills* Using signposting language Introducing examples Expressing general beliefs *Pronunciation* Signposting phrases *Speaking Task* Give a two-minute presentation about the human threats to an endangered species.	*Communication Skill* Making yourself understood
Negative prefixes Modals to express future possibility	Analyzing opinions Forming arguments and counterarguments	*Speaking Skills* Linking ideas with transition words and phrases Talking about advantages and disadvantages Giving counterarguments *Speaking Task* Take part in a debate. Argue for or against building a new shopping center in your city.	*Study Skill* Active learning
Talking about problems and solutions Comparative and superlative adjectives	Evaluating problems Proposing solutions	*Speaking Skills* Giving recommendations Expanding on an idea *Speaking Task* Give a presentation on a transportation problem and suggest solutions to solve the problem.	*Life Skill* Setting SMART goals
Suffixes Dependent prepositions	Analyzing positives and negatives	*Speaking Skills* Being polite in a discussion Using adverbs for emphasis Phrases with *that* *Pronunciation* Stress patterns in phrases for agreeing and disagreeing *Speaking Task* Take part in a discussion about whether special occasions have become too commercial.	*Life Skill* Dealing with culture shock

UNIT	WATCH AND LISTEN	LISTENINGS	LISTENING SKILLS	PRONUNCIATION FOR LISTENING	
5 HEALTH AND FITNESS *Academic Disciplines* Health Science / Sports Management	Yoga in California Schools	1: A radio program about why some people life a long life 2: Four presentations about programs to improve your health	*Key Skills* Listening for attitude Identifying references to common knowledge *Additional Skills* Understanding key vocabulary Using your knowledge Listening for main ideas Listening for details Taking notes Synthesizing	Intonation: expressing attitude and emotion	
6 DISCOVERY AND INVENTION *Academic Disciplines* Art and Design / History	A Helping Hand	1: A museum tour about inventions in the Middle Ages 2: A lecture about the history of smartphone apps	*Key Skills* Understanding references to earlier ideas Understanding lecture organization *Additional Skills* Understanding key vocabulary Using your knowledge Listening for main ideas Listening for details Listening for text organization Taking notes Synthesizing	Weak and strong forms	
7 FASHION *Academic Disciplines* Business / Fashion Design / Marketing	The Growth of Louis Vuitton	1: A discussion about clothes of the future 2: An interview with a fashion designer	*Key Skills* Taking notes on main ideas and details Identifying auxiliary verbs for emphasis *Additional Skills* Understanding key vocabulary Using your knowledge Listening for main ideas Listening for details Making inferences Synthesizing	Vowel omission	
8 ECONOMICS *Academic Disciplines* Business / Economics / Sociology	Workshops for Entrepreneurs	1: A radio program about a book about millionaire lifestyles 2: A discussion about whether college students should be paid for good grades	*Key Skill* Understanding paraphrases *Additional Skills* Understanding key vocabulary Using your knowledge Listening for main ideas Listening for details Listening for opinion Taking notes Synthesizing	Silent letters	

LANGUAGE DEVELOPMENT	CRITICAL THINKING	SPEAKING	ON CAMPUS
Phrasal verbs Adjectives to describe well-being	Brainstorming and evaluating ideas using idea maps	***Speaking Skills*** Problem-solution organization Presenting persuasively ***Speaking Task*** Give a presentation to a group of students about an idea for a health product or program.	***Life Skill*** Staying in shape
Uses of the verb *make* Passive verb forms	Researching a topic using *Wh-* questions and idea maps	***Speaking Skills*** Previewing a topic Organizing ideas Explaining how something is used ***Speaking Task*** Give a presentation about an invention or discovery that has changed our lives.	***Presentation Skill*** Using visuals
Idioms Predictions and expectations about the future	Analyzing and creating purpose statements and interview questions	***Speaking Skills*** Asking for opinions and checking information Asking follow-up questions ***Speaking Task*** Take part in an interview to find out attitudes about uniforms and dress codes.	***Study Skill*** Planning assignments
Collocations with *pay* and *money* Present and future real conditionals	Identifying and evaluating reasons for and against an idea	***Speaking Skills*** Using gerunds as subjects to talk about actions Presenting reasons and evidence to support an argument Using paraphrases ***Speaking Task*** Take part in a discussion about whether young people should be allowed to have credit cards.	***Communication Skill*** Meeting your academic advisor

1 Video

Setting the context

Every unit begins with a video clip. Each video serves as a springboard for the unit and introduces the topic in an engaging way. The clips were carefully selected to pique students' interest and prepare them to explore the unit's topic in greater depth. As they work, students develop key skills in prediction, comprehension, and discussion.

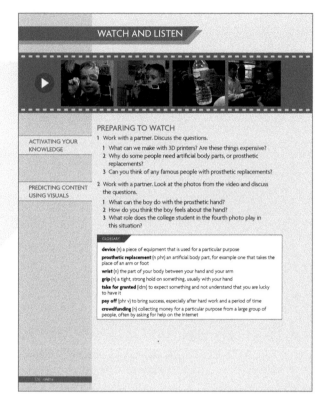

WATCH AND LISTEN

ACTIVATING YOUR KNOWLEDGE

PREDICTING CONTENT USING VISUALS

PREPARING TO WATCH

1 Work with a partner. Discuss the questions.
1 What can we make with 3D printers? Are these things expensive?
2 Why do some people need artificial body parts, or prosthetic replacements?
3 Can you think of any famous people with prosthetic replacements?

2 Work with a partner. Look at the photos from the video and discuss the questions.
1 What can the boy do with the prosthetic hand?
2 How do you think the boy feels about the hand?
3 What role does the college student in the fourth photo play in this situation?

GLOSSARY

device (n) a piece of equipment that is used for a particular purpose
prosthetic replacement (n phr) an artificial body part, for example one that takes the place of an arm or foot
wrist (n) the part of your body between your hand and your arm
grip (n) a tight, strong hold on something, usually with your hand
take for granted (idm) to expect something and not understand that you are lucky to have it
pay off (phr v) to bring success, especially after hard work and a period of time
crowdfunding (n) collecting money for a particular purpose from a large group of people, often by asking for help on the Internet

2 Listening

Receptive, language, and analytical skills

Students improve their listening abilities through a sequence of proven activities. They study key vocabulary to prepare them for each listening and to develop academic listening skills. Pronunciation for Listening exercises help students learn how to decode spoken English. Language Development sections teach grammar and vocabulary. A second listening leads into synthesis exercises that prepare students for college classrooms.

WHILE LISTENING

LISTENING FOR MAIN IDEAS

4 1.1 Listen to the debate again and complete the chart. What are the animals used for?

	protection	building	transportation	war
dogs	✔			
horses				
elephants				
camels				

Taking notes

Taking notes while listening will make you a more active listener. There are many ways to take notes while listening. One way to take notes is by using a T-chart. T-charts can help you organize information into two aspects of a topic, such as pros and cons or facts and opinions.

Using Animals for Work

cons (against)	pros (for)
it's cruel	helps poor people

5 1.1 Listen to the debate again. What are Ms. Johnson's and Dr. Kuryan's opinions on animal rights? Complete the student's notes in the T-chart using words from the box.

cruel   poor   rights   skills   survive   technology

TAKING NOTES ON OPINION

PRISM Online Workbook

con (Ms. Johnson's ideas)	pro (Dr. Kuryan's ideas)
1 We have technology that can replace animals.	4
2	5
3	6

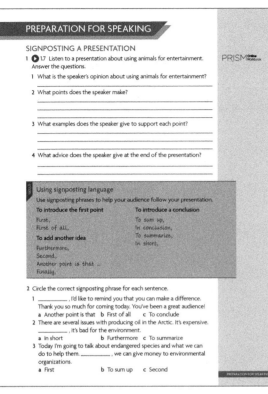

3 Speaking

Critical thinking and production

Multiple critical thinking activities begin this section, setting students up for exercises that focus on speaking skills, functional language, and pronunciation. All of these lead up to a structured speaking task, in which students apply the skills and language they have developed over the course of the entire unit.

4 On Campus

Skills for college life

This unique section teaches students valuable skills beyond academic listening and speaking. From asking questions in class to participating in a study group and from being an active listener to finding help, students learn how to navigate university life. The section begins with a context-setting listening, and moves directly into active practice of the skill.

ON CAMPUS

DEALING WITH CULTURE SHOCK

PREPARING TO LISTEN

1 You are going to listen to three students describing problems they had when they first arrived in North America to study. Before you listen, work in a small group and discuss the problems that students might have. What kinds of problems do you think international students might have with the following?

> classes   cultural behavior   food   language   weather

WHILE LISTENING

2 ▶ 4.11 Listen to the students' descriptions. Circle the topics in Exercise 1 that you hear.

3 ▶ 4.11 Listen to the descriptions again and circle the correct ending for each sentence.

1 Alisha was most upset because she couldn't _____.
a understand anything.
b say what she wanted to.
c take notes.

2 In her English classes, Alisha learned how to _____.
a make friends.
b speak English better.
c study in English.

3 John didn't like American food because _____.
a it made him sick.
b it was too sweet.
c it was too unhealthy.

4 Now John _____.
a likes American food.
b likes cheese.
c still eats Chinese food.

5 Minh thought that Americans _____.
a did not mean what they said.
b were not polite.
c were not friendly.

4 Work in a small group and discuss the questions.
1 How did each student manage to resolve their problem?
2 Have you ever had an experience like Alisha's, John's, or Minh's? If so, describe it.

WHAT MAKES *PRISM* SPECIAL: CRITICAL THINKING

Bloom's Taxonomy

In order to truly prepare for college coursework, students need to develop a full range of thinking skills. *Prism* teaches explicit critical thinking skills in every unit of every level. These skills adhere to the taxonomy developed by Benjamin Bloom. By working within the taxonomy, we are able to ensure that your students learn both lower-order and higher-order thinking skills.

Critical thinking exercises are accompanied by icons indicating where the activities fall in Bloom's Taxonomy.

SPEAKING

CRITICAL THINKING

At the end of this unit, you will do the Speaking Task below.

Give a presentation to a group of students about an idea for a health product or program.

Using idea maps

Idea maps are a good way to organize your notes as you listen. They help you see connections between the topic, the main ideas, and the details.

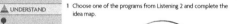

△ UNDERSTAND

1 Choose one of the programs from Listening 2 and complete the idea map.

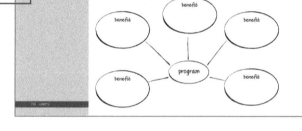

Create: create, invent, plan, compose, construct, design, imagine

Evaluate: decide, rate, choose, recommend, justify, assess, prioritize

Analyze: explain, contrast, examine, identify, investigate, categorize

Apply: show, complete, use, classify, illustrate, solve

Understand: compare, discuss, restate, predict, translate, outline

Remember: name, describe, relate, find, list, write, tell

3 Write all of the ideas your group discussed in the chart.

Special occasions have become too commercial.	Special occasions have not become too commercial.

4 Decide which side of the debate you agree with. List the three main reasons for your opinion.

EVALUATE

Reason 1: _____

Reason 2: _____

Reason 3: _____

PREPARATION FOR SPEAKING

BEING POLITE IN A DISCUSSION

To have a good discussion, it is important to say when you agree and disagree with people. When you disagree, show that you understand and respect the other person's opinion.
You may be right, but ...
I see your point, but ...
You should also take turns and ask other peoples' opinions. You can do this by asking questions.
What do you think?
What's your opinion?
If you want to interrupt someone because you have a point to make, you can do it politely.
I'm sorry to interrupt, but ...
Excuse me for interrupting, but ...
Excuse me, can I say something?

PREPARATION FOR SPEAKING 95

Higher-Order Thinking Skills

Create, **Evaluate**, and **Analyze** are critical skills for students in any college setting. Academic success depends on their abilities to derive knowledge from collected data, make educated judgments, and deliver insightful presentations. *Prism* helps students get there by creating activities such as categorizing information, comparing data, selecting the best solution to a problem, and developing arguments for a discussion or presentation.

3 Work alone. Make a list of the advantages and disadvantages of allowing young people to have credit cards.

EVALUATE

advantages
1 _____
2 _____
3 _____
4 _____
disadvantages
1 _____
2 _____
3 _____
4 _____

4 Work with a partner and discuss your ideas from Exercise 3.

5 Work alone. Decide which side of the argument you support. Complete the chart with your three best arguments for each side. Add supporting details for each argument.

APPLY

arguments that support the position	arguments that oppose the position
Argument 1: Supporting details:	Argument 1: Supporting details:
Argument 2: Supporting details:	Argument 2: Supporting details:

CRITICAL THINKING 183

Lower-Order Thinking Skills

Apply, **Understand**, and **Remember** provide the foundation upon which all thinking occurs. Students need to be able to recall information, comprehend it, and see its use in new contexts. *Prism* develops these skills through exercises such as taking notes, mining notes for specific data, demonstrating comprehension, and distilling information from charts.

WHAT MAKES *PRISM* SPECIAL:
ON CAMPUS

More college skills

Students need more than traditional academic skills. *Prism* teaches important skills for being engaged and successful all around campus, from emailing professors to navigating study groups.

Professors

Students learn how to take good lecture notes and how to communicate with professors and academic advisors.

Beyond the classroom

Skills include how to utilize campus resources, where to go for help, how to choose classes, and more.

Active learning

Students practice participating in class, in online discussion boards, and in study groups.

Texts

Learners become proficient at taking notes and annotating textbooks as well as conducting research online and in the library.

LISTENING 2

PREPARING TO LISTEN

UNDERSTANDING
KEY VOCABULARY

PRISM Online Workbook

1 You are going to listen to a debate about nuclear power. Before you listen, read the information about wind power. Complete the definitions with the correct form of the words in bold.

Many people think wind power has many **benefits**. First, it is environmentally friendly; it does not **pollute** the environment. Also, unlike coal mines and nuclear power plants, it is unlikely to cause accidents and never leads to **disasters**. Therefore, there is a very low **risk** of danger. Most importantly, this source of energy is **affordable**. However, **opponents** of wind power argue that the wind turbines can have a negative effect on the environment. They say that a turbine takes up a lot of space. Another point is that the wind turbines are not a **long-term** source of energy, unlike nuclear power plants.

1 _benefits_ (n) advantages
2 _____ (n) the possibility of something bad happening
3 _____ (adj) continuing for a long time
4 _____ (n) terrible accidents that cause a lot of damage
5 _____ (adj) not expensive
6 _____ (n) people who disagree with an idea
7 _____ (v) to make something, like air or water, dirty or harmful

46 UNIT 2

Vocabulary Research

Learning the right words

Students need to learn a wide range of general and academic vocabulary in order to be successful in college. *Prism* carefully selects the vocabulary that students study based on the General Service List, the Academic Word List, and the Cambridge English Corpus.

PRONUNCIATION FOR LISTENING

Connected speech: /t/ and /d/ at the end of words

When people speak quickly and naturally, the gaps between words are often not easy to hear, and people don't always pronounce all the letters in a word. For example, they don't always pronounce the /t/ or /d/ sounds at the end of words if they are part of a cluster of consonants.

Listen to this sentence. The letters highlighted in green are not pronounced clearly. The letter highlighted in yellow is pronounced clearly.

▶ 4.4 I study different cultures around the world and how social and political changes affect these cultures.

PRISM Online Workbook

9 ▶ 4.5 Listen to excerpts from the program. Circle the /t/ and /d/ sounds that you can hear clearly in the bold words. In one sentence you don't need to circle any sounds.

1 My book is **about** the **effect** of modern technology on traditions **around** the world.
2 People **spent** a lot of time and **effort** preparing special meals.
3 Growing up in **different** cultures helps you realize **that** customs and traditions are often local.
4 We still **spend** time interacting with other people, **but** it's **not** always face-to-face.
5 In the **past**, people **sent** each other cards to celebrate **important** events like birthdays and anniversaries.
6 Traditions **don't** always die out – **but** customs and traditions do change **and adapt** to the modern world.

DISCUSSION

10 Work in a small group. Discuss the questions.

1 Think about the important traditions in your country. Are they still relevant today? Why or why not?
2 Do you know any traditions that have disappeared since your grandparents were young? Why do you think they disappeared?
3 What are some traditions or customs that have changed over the last 20 years? Why have they changed?

88 UNIT 4

Pronunciation for Listening

Training your ears

This unique feature teaches learners to listen for specific features of spoken English that typically inhibit comprehension. Learners become primed to better understand detail and nuance while listening.

Listening skills	Take notes; listen for contrasting ideas; listen for signposting language
Pronunciation	Intonation of lists; stress in signposting phrases
Speaking skills	Use signposting language in a presentation; introduce examples; express general beliefs
Speaking Task	Give a presentation
On Campus	Make yourself understood

cats have a strange caracttrea

verb

ACTIVATE YOUR KNOWLEDGE

Work with a partner. Discuss the questions.

is

pulling a cars

1 Look at the photo. What work are the dogs doing?

2 Are animals used for work in your country? If yes, what work do they do?

3 What other types of work can animals do?

WATCH AND LISTEN

PREPARING TO WATCH

ACTIVATING YOUR KNOWLEDGE

1 Work with a partner. Discuss the questions.

1 Can animals solve problems? Give examples.
2 How do animals play? Do you think they like puzzles or games? Why or why not?

PREDICTING CONTENT USING VISUALS

2 Work with a partner. Look at the photos from the video and discuss the questions.

1 What is the goal of a game like a maze?
2 In your opinion, is the chimpanzee thinking? Why or why not?
3 Do you think the chimpanzee and the man are happy or angry? Explain your answer.

GLOSSARY

mental (adj) related to the mind or the process of thinking

maze (n) a type of puzzle with a series of paths from entrance to exit

in the wild (p phr) in nature, not in a zoo, on a farm, or as a pet

reflect upon (phr v) to think about in a serious and careful way

---

WHILE WATCHING

UNDERSTANDING MAIN IDEAS

3 ▶ Watch the video. Circle the correct answers.

1 The scientists wanted to find out if chimpanzees could _____ .
   a look for food
   b plan ahead
   c protect themselves
2 The chimpanzee is able to _____ .
   a use a computer
   b ask for food
   c listen to commands

3 The goal of the game is to _____ .
   a climb the stairs
   b eat the cherries
   (c) find the exit

4 Sometimes Panzee, the chimpanzee, can see the solution to the maze
   faster than _____ can.
   (a) a human
   b a computer
   c the scientist

5 According to the professor, chimpanzees are able to _____ .
   (a) communicate
   b make plans
   c think faster than people

4 ▶ Watch the video again. Write *T* (true), *F* (false), or *DNS* (does not say)
   next to the statements. Then, correct the false statements.

   _F_ 1 In the wild, chimpanzees have to look for friends.
   _____

   _T_ 2 Panzee can often complete mazes that she has never
          seen before.
   _____

   _F_ 3 Planning before acting is just a human skill.
                                Not
   _____

   _T_ 4 The scientist says that chimpanzees reflect upon the past.
   _____

   _F_ 5 Chimpanzees can plan ahead for centuries. day
   _____

DISCUSSION

5 Work in a small group. Discuss the questions. Then, compare your answers
  with another group.

   1 Make a list of five animals that are very smart.
   2 For each animal you chose, give an example of its intelligence.
   3 Do animals remember things? Give reasons and examples for
     your answer.

LISTENING 1

PREPARING TO LISTEN

UNDERSTANDING KEY VOCABULARY

1 You are going to listen to a debate about using animals for work. Before you listen, read the definitions. Complete the sentences with the correct form of the words in bold.

> **abuse** (n) violent or unfair treatment of someone
> **conditions** (n) the situation in which someone lives or works
> **cruel** (adj) not kind
> **issue** (n) a topic or problem that causes concern and discussion
> **protect** (v) to keep safe from danger
> **suffer** (v) to feel pain or unhappiness
> **survive** (v) to continue to live, in spite of danger and difficulty
> **welfare** (n) someone's or something's health and happiness

1 Some people feel that using elephants in the circus is animal _abuse_. To be healthy, elephants need to live in the wild.
2 This animal organization helps to _protect_ animals that are in danger. It saves thousands of animals every year.
3 People who let animals go hungry are _cruel_. I don't understand how they can be so mean.
4 Some wild animals _suffer_ in zoos. They live in small, uncomfortable cages, and they don't have enough space to run.
5 The _conditions_ in this zoo are excellent. All of the animals have plenty of space and are treated very well.
6 The biggest _issue_ for many animal rights organizations is the use of animals in scientific experiments.
7 Sharks continue to _survive_ in the ocean, as they have for about 450 million years, despite the threat from humans.
8 There are laws that protect the _welfare_ of animals by making sure humans are punished for hurting them.

USING YOUR KNOWLEDGE

2 Work with a partner. Discuss the questions.

1 What are some reasons in favor of using animals for work?
2 What are some reasons against using animals for work?

3 ▶ 1.1 Listen to the debate and check your answers.

WHILE LISTENING

4 ▶ 1.1 Listen to the debate again and complete the chart. What are the animals used for?

	protection	building	transportation	war
dogs	✔	✓	✓	
horses			✓	✓
elephants		✓	✓	
camels		✓	✓	✓

SKILLS

Taking notes

Taking notes while listening will make you a more active listener. There are many ways to take notes while listening. One way to take notes is by using a T-chart. T-charts can help you organize information into two aspects of a topic, such as pros and cons or facts and opinions.

Using Animals for Work

cons (against)	pros (for)
it's cruel	helps poor people

5 ▶ 1.1 Listen to the debate again. What are Ms. Johnson's and Dr. Kuryan's opinions on animal rights? Complete the student's notes in the T-chart using words from the box.

PRISM Online Workbook

cruel   poor   rights   skills   survive   ~~technology~~

con (Ms. Johnson's ideas)	pro (Dr. Kuryan's ideas)
1 We have technology that can replace animals.	4 coward donky helping Poor People
2 deception skills	5
3 who ation is hungry he is cruel to pets	6

POST-LISTENING

Listening for contrasting ideas

Speakers use certain words and phrases to signal a contrast, or difference, between two ideas. To identify contrasting ideas, listen for these transition words and phrases: *yet, but, on the contrary, even though, however.*

Animals, like elephants and horses, were used to build amazing structures, like the pyramids in Egypt. **Yet/But** their hard work and suffering are hardly ever recognized.

Not all animal use is abuse. **On the contrary**, without humans, these domesticated animals would not have been able to survive.

Even though animals work hard for us, they are often abandoned when they get sick or too old to work.

These animals work long hours and live in difficult conditions. **However,** they get very little reward.

LISTENING FOR TEXT ORGANIZATION

PRISM Online Workbook

6 Circle the correct contrasting transition words and phrases.

1 *Even though* / *However* I love animals, I don't think people should keep them in their homes.

2 Some people think the reason I became a vegetarian is because I love animals. *Even though* / *On the contrary*, I am a vegetarian for health reasons, and not because I care about animal rights.

3 Many people are against animal testing. *Even though* / *Yet,* without such tests, we would not have developed new medicines.

4 *Even though* / *Yet* people claim that animal rights aren't protected, there are many organizations all over the world that focus on this issue.

5 Many people eat meat. *Yet* / *On the contrary*, humans don't need animal protein to stay healthy.

7 Complete the excerpts with the transition words and phrases in the box.
Sometimes more than one answer is possible.

> but   even though   however   on the contrary   yet

1 People talk a lot about protecting animals, _____ *yet* _____
   they often don't do anything to help the animals.
2 Zoos are fun places for children to visit, *however* / *but*, some
   zoos do not provide good living conditions for their animals.
3 _____ *even though* _____, I like animals, I wouldn't want to be
   a veterinarian.
4 Most people aren't cruel to animals, *on the contrary*, they care
   a lot about animal welfare.

DISCUSSION

8 Read the statements. Do you agree or disagree with them? Work alone
and make notes. Think of reasons for your opinion.

1 In the modern world, there is no longer any need to use animals for
   work. We have developed technology that can replace them. Using
   animals for work is similar to using children to work in factories.
2 People often spend too much time and money on animals. They
   should focus less on helping animals and more on helping poor people.

9 Work in a group of three. Discuss your opinions.

عائلة الكلمات

WORD FAMILIES

LANGUAGE

You can develop your academic vocabulary by working on word families. Word families often start with the same letters and end differently, depending on the form. When you record a new word in your notebook, make sure to write down any other forms from its word family. If you don't know a word, you may be able to guess it from another form of the word.

PRISM Online Workbook

1 Complete the chart. Sometimes there is more than one possible answer. Use a dictionary to help you.

noun	verb	adjective	adverb
abandonment			
	abuse	abused	abusively
analysis	analyze	analytical	analytically
communication		communced	communicatively
	connect		
damage	damage	damaged	
debate	debate	debatebol	
environment		environmedl	
involvement	involve	involved	involvedly
protection	protecti	proteckied	protectively
support	support	supported	supportively
survivor / survival	survive	survivol	

2 Complete the sentences with the correct form of the words in parentheses.

1 The _____analysis_____ of the blood sample showed that the horse was healthy. (analyze)

2 Domesticated animals may find it very hard to _____survive_____ in the wild. (survive)

3 Owners sometimes _abandon_ their animals on the street when they can no longer take care of them. (abandon)

4 She is a strong _supporter_ of animal rights. (support)

5 Using _environmentaly_ damaging chemicals on farms can endanger wild animals as well as plants. (environment)

6 Some scientists have explored how birds _communicat_ with each other by using different sounds. (communicate)

7 She has had a lot of _involvment_ with animal rights for the last 25 years. (involve)

8 Many people are very _protective_ toward animals, and they want to take care of them. (protect)

9 I listened to a _debate_ about animal rights. (debate)

10 Many people who are _abusively_ to animals aren't that way on purpose. (abuse)

MODALS FOR NECESSITY AND ADVICE

Use *have to, have got to, need to,* or *must* before a verb to say that something is necessary.*

Animals **have to / have got to / need to / must** find food, water, and a safe place to live in order to survive.

Use *don't have to / don't need to* to say that something isn't necessary.

You **don't have to / don't need to** feed the chickens. I already fed them.

Use *should* or *ought to* to give advice.

You **should / ought to** give some money to that animal rights organization. It does good work.

* *Must* is often used in writing to express rules and laws, and is rare in speaking.

3 Look at the sentences and the underlined modals. What does each sentence express? Write *necessity* or *advice* next to each sentence.

1 You <u>have to</u> love animals to be a vet. _necessary_

2 You <u>should not</u> give human food to animals. _advice_

3 What courses do you <u>need to</u> complete to get a veterinary degree? _necessary_

4 You <u>ought to</u> visit the San Diego Zoo. It has some really interesting animals. _advice_

4 Circle the sentence that best matches each picture.

1 **a** We have to wear a uniform.
   b We shouldn't wear a uniform.

2 **a** You shouldn't park here.
   b You don't have to park here.

3 **a** You've got to buy a ticket.
   b You don't need to buy a ticket.

4 **a** He shouldn't wear this to work.
   b He doesn't need to wear this to work.

PREPARING TO LISTEN

UNDERSTANDING
KEY VOCABULARY

PRISM Online Workbook

1 You are going to listen to a presentation about human threats to polar bears. Before you listen, read the sentences and circle the best definition for the word or phrase in bold.

1 Climate change is causing ice in the oceans to **melt**.
   a to become liquid as a result of heating
   b to get colder

2 Some species of bat are in danger because plants, their biggest food **source**, are sprayed with dangerous chemicals.
   a the cause of something
   b where something comes from

3 Polar bears are **endangered**. If we don't do something to save them, they will probably disappear.
   a at risk of no longer existing
   b very dangerous

4 Most people have only seen lions in a zoo or animal park, and not in their own **habitat** in the African savannah.
   a the natural environment of an animal or plant
   b a building where animals live

5 There are two **species** of elephants: Asian elephants and African elephants.
   a animals that are both under threat
   b a group of plants or animals that share similar features

6 Polar bears **depend on** sea ice for survival. Without the ice, it's difficult for them to hunt for seals.
   a to need
   b to have

7 Oil spills can **damage** the polar bear's environment and can even kill them.
   a to hurt
   b to help

8 Human **threats** to the environment include climate change, deforestation, and pollution.
   a the possibility of trouble, danger, or disaster
   b suggestions for improvement

2 Look at the photos and answer the questions.

1 What do you think is happening in the photos?
2 What threats do you think the speaker will talk about?
3 Can you think of any other threats to polar bears?

[handwritten: Pollion annal hunting]

3 ▶ 1.2 Listen to the presentation. Were your ideas mentioned?

[handwritten: thinks]

WHILE LISTENING

4 ▶ 1.2 Listen to the presentation again and complete the notes.

human threats to polar bears	what people are doing to help polar bears
1 loss of sea ice habitat	4 *You should use Less electricity and ges*
2 *Contact between humans and Polar bears*	5 *tell goverment leades and get involved with organizitions*
3 *Industrial development.*	6

5 ▶ 1.2 Complete the sentences. Then, listen to check your answers.

1 There are only about *26,000* polar bears in the world today.
2 Most polar bears will probably be gone by *2050* if nothing changes.
3 The sea ice is disappearing for longer periods of time every *summer* .
4 When polar bears go near *towns* , people sometimes kill the bears to protect themselves.
5 Groups are creating plans to make Arctic shipping *safer* .
6 If you want to help save polar bears, you should use less electricity and *gas* .

POST-LISTENING

LISTENING FOR TEXT
ORGANIZATION

> **SKILLS**
>
> ## Listening for signposting language
>
> When you listen to a presentation, listen for signposting phrases (*first, second, to summarize*). These phrases are like road signs – they help you know when a speaker is moving to a new point or section.

6 ▶ 1.3 Listen to excerpts from the presentation and write the signposting phrases you hear.

1 _____first_____ , Arctic communities are trying to reduce contact between humans and polar bears.

2 _____second_____ , governments have made laws that prohibit or limit the amount of oil production in the Arctic.

3 So, _to summarize_ the main threat to polar bears is loss of habitat due to climate change.

PRONUNCIATION FOR LISTENING

> **SKILLS**
>
> ## Intonation of lists
>
> Speakers often list examples of what they are talking about. Giving a list of examples can help persuade the audience. These lists have their own intonation patterns. Speakers pause between each example in the list and stress each word.
>
> If the list is complete, the last example in the list has falling intonation, like this:
>
> ▶ 1.4 … _beautiful_ ↗, _powerful_ ↗, _majestic_ ↘
>
> If the list is not complete, the last example has rising intonation, like this:
>
> ▶ 1.5 … _warmer_ _temperatures_ ↗, _floods_ ↗, _droughts_ ↗, _huge_ _storms_ … ↗
>
> When you are taking notes, it is important to listen for this intonation so you know that the list isn't complete yet.

7 ▶ 1.6 Listen to the lists. Is each list complete or not complete? Check the correct answer.

	complete	not complete
1 large, white, strong		✓
2 pandas, sea turtles, chimpanzees, tigers	✓	
3 human contact, climate change, industrial development	✓	
4 more lights, electric fences, warning plans		✓

8 ▶ 1.6 Listen to the lists again. Practice saying each list with rising and falling intonation.

DISCUSSION

SYNTHESIZING

9 Work in a small group. Think about Listening 1 and Listening 2 and answer the questions.

1 Do you think humans should be responsible for protecting animals? Why or why not? *Yes, because we are responsable for the damge*

2 There are about 8.7 million species on Earth. Does it matter if some of them become extinct? Why or why not?

3 Besides the ideas that the speaker mentions, can you think of other ways to help protect endangered species? Which of the ways is the easiest? Which is the most effective? Why?

① protecting animals from human danger

3)

in i

② yes, because every species has advantages for the earth.

③ stop polluting the environment.

SPEAKING

CRITICAL THINKING

At the end of this unit, you are going to do the Speaking Task below.

Give a two-minute presentation about the human threats to an endangered species.

UNDERSTAND

1 Think about Listening 2 and circle the correct answer.

1 Who is the audience? Who is the speaker talking to?
   - a scientists
   - (b) college students

2 What is the speaker's most important objective, or purpose?
   - (a) to inform the audience about human threats to the polar bear
   - b to teach the audience about polar bears' habits

2 The speaker in Listening 2 used this chart to plan his presentation. Complete the chart. Use information from your notes on page 26.

main idea	Polar Bears are threatened by humans.
supporting details	Threats: • loss of sea ice habitat • 26 [illegible] • What people are doing to help: • 4 reduce contact between humans and Polar bear • 5 government have pro the amount of oil production hited • 6 [illegible] People are trying to stop climate change
conclusion/ summary	To summarize, the main threat to Polar bears losse of habitat due to climate change. Related threats are human contact and industrial development. if People dont make changes quickly, Polar Pears may disappear

3 Choose an endangered species to talk about. Use one of the species in the box or choose another. Complete the planning chart for your presentation.

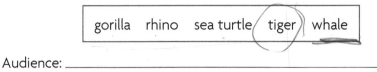

| gorilla | rhino | sea turtle | tiger | whale |

Audience: _____

Objective: _____

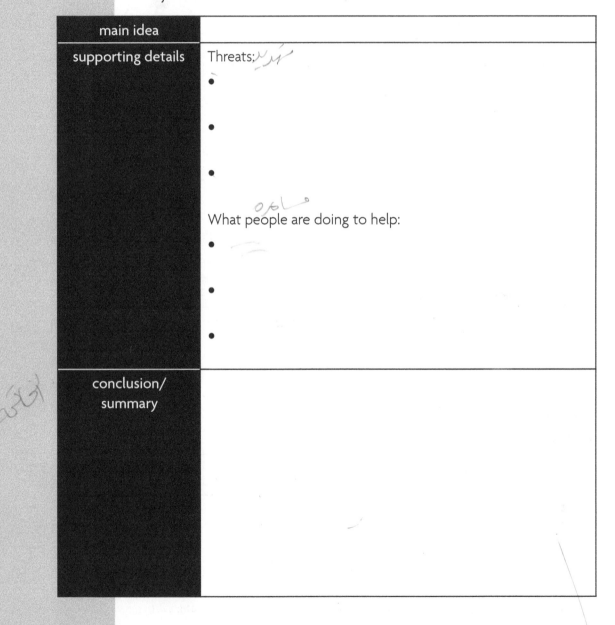

main idea	
supporting details	Threats: • • • What people are doing to help: • • •
conclusion/ summary	

PREPARATION FOR SPEAKING

SIGNPOSTING A PRESENTATION

1 ▶ 1.7 Listen to a presentation about using animals for entertainment. Answer the questions.

1 What is the speaker's opinion about using animals for entertainment?
   his opinion is it is ok

2 What points does the speaker make?
   ① Keeping animals in zoo helps protecting them

3 What examples does the speaker give to support each point?
   the

4 What advice does the speaker give at the end of the presentation?

SKILLS

Using signposting language

Use signposting phrases to help your audience follow your presentation.

To introduce the first point

First,
First of all,

To add another idea

Furthermore,
Second,
Another point is that ...
Finally,

To introduce a conclusion

To sum up,
In conclusion,
To summarize,
In short,

---

2 Circle the correct signposting phrase for each sentence.

1 _____ , I'd like to remind you that you can make a difference. Thank you so much for coming today. You've been a great audience!
   a Another point is that   **b First of all**   c To conclude

2 There are several issues with producing oil in the Arctic. It's expensive. _____ , it's bad for the environment.
   a In short   **b Furthermore**   c To summarize

3 Today I'm going to talk about endangered species and what we can do to help them. _____ , we can give money to environmental organizations.
   a First   b To sum up   c Second

Introducing examples

Speakers also use signposting phrases (*for instance, for example, such as*) to introduce examples.

Another point is that zoos have an important educational role.
For instance, *children can see animals up close.*
Keeping animals in zoos helps protect them. **For example**, *many species,* **such as** *the giant panda and the snow leopard, are endangered.*

3 Work with a partner. Add your own examples to these points.

1 I think that zoos are sometimes good for animals. For example, _They_ _can protect endangered animals_ .

2 You can see many exotic animals in zoos, such as _snakes_ _____ .

3 Animals are sometimes unhappy in zoos. For instance, _they live_ _in small cages_ .

Expressing general beliefs

In a presentation, use phrases like *It's believed that* ... to talk about what most people think or believe. This shows that the idea is not only your idea.

It's often said that *it's cruel to use animals for entertainment.*
It's believed that *most of the polar bears will be gone by 2050 if nothing changes.*
It's widely known that *climate change is a threat to polar bears.*

4 Work with a partner. Complete the sentences with your own ideas.

1 It's often said that _zoos are bad for animals_ .
2 It's believed that _animals are always suffer in zoos_ .
3 It's widely known that _____ .

PRONUNCIATION FOR SPEAKING

5 ▶ 1.8 Listen to the excerpts. Notice how the signposting phrases in bold are pronounced as one complete phrase. Underline the stressed word in each signposting phrase.

1 <u>First</u> of all, keeping animals in zoos helps protect them.
2 For <u>example</u>, many species, such as the giant panda and the snow leopard, are endangered in the wild.
3 <u>Another</u> point is that zoos have an important educational role.
4 To <u>summarize</u>, zoos help protect animals and educate us.
5 In <u>short</u>, modern zoos are comfortable, safe places for wild animals.

6 ▶ 1.8 Listen to the excerpts again and practice saying the sentences.

SPEAKING TASK

Give a two-minute presentation about the human threats to an endangered species.

PREPARE

1 Look at the presentation plan you created in Exercise 3 in Critical Thinking. Review your notes and add any new information.

2 Use the Task Checklist to prepare your presentation.

3 Prepare some notes about your introduction.

4 For each supporting detail in your plan, make notes about the language you will use.

5 Prepare a concluding statement. Say what people should do to save the species.

TASK CHECKLIST	✔
Use transition words and phrases to contrast ideas. *20*	
Use modals for necessity and advice. *23*	
Use appropriate intonation in lists. *27*	
Support your points with examples. *32*	
Use appropriate signposting language. *31*	

PRACTICE

6 Work in a group of three. Take turns practicing your presentations. Then, discuss the questions below. Take notes during the discussion.

1 Did the speaker clearly identify each threat to the species?
2 Did the speaker use signposting phrases to help the listener?
3 Did the speaker use examples to support points?
4 How could the speaker improve the presentation?

PRESENT

7 Take turns giving your presentations to the class.

ON CAMPUS

MAKING YOURSELF UNDERSTOOD

PREPARING TO LISTEN

1 You are going to listen to a lecture about giving presentations. Before you listen, read the advice below and check the strategies that you agree with.

When giving a presentation in front of a class, you should ...		
	you	the professor
1 read your presentation aloud.		
2 memorize what you will say.		
3 use notes.		
4 practice pronunciation of important words.		
5 shout.		
6 say important points more clearly and slowly.		
7 use signposting language.		

2 Work with a partner. Compare your answers. Which of the strategies above make it easier for your audience to understand you?

WHILE LISTENING

3 ▶ 1.9 Listen to the lecture. Check the strategies that the professor mentions. Did you choose the same strategies?

4 ▶ 1.9 Listen to the lecture again and answer the questions. Then, compare your answers with a partner.

1 According to the professor, what happens when students read or memorize presentations?

_____

2 What happens when you use notes?

_____

3 What kind of words should you practice pronouncing?

_____

4 When should you pause?

_____

5 What are some examples of signposting language?

_____

Strategies to help your audience understand you

When you are speaking in front of the class, use strategies to help your audience understand you.

- don't read aloud; use notes
- make sure you can pronounce key words
- say important points clearly and slowly
- pause after each point
- use signposting language

PRACTICE

5 Look at the script for audio 1.1 on pages 194–195. Complete the notes using the words in the box.

> building Dogs food thousands transportation

(1)_____ = oldest domesticated animal

Others: sheep, cows, goats, horses, camels, elephants

These animals have worked for humans for (2)_____ of years

How have humans used animals?

Sheep, cows, goats: (3)_____

Horses, camels & elephants:
- transportation
- (4)_____ (pyramids)
- farming (pulling heavy machinery) and logging (elephants)

Dogs:
- (5)_____ (e.g., dog sleds in Alaska today)
- security (e.g., guard dogs)

6 Underline the important words in the notes. Then, practice pronouncing them.

7 Work in a small group. Practice giving a presentation based on the notes. Remember to speak slowly and clearly, pause, and use signposting language.

REAL-WORLD APPLICATION

8 Prepare a one-minute presentation about one of the topics below.

> how animals are important in my life   the job of a veterinarian
> why I am (not) a vegetarian   why I am studying English

9 Work in a small group and give your presentations. After your presentation, ask your group whether you did everything from the box above. Was there anything you missed?

Listening skills	Listen for explanations; listen for counterarguments
Pronunciation	Connected speech: linking sounds
Speaking skills	Link ideas with transition words and phrases; talk about advantages and disadvantages; give counterarguments
Speaking Task	Take part in a debate
On Campus	Active learning

THE ENVIRONMENT

ACTIVATE YOUR KNOWLEDGE

Work with a partner. Discuss the questions.

1 Look at the photo of solar panels. What do you know about this energy source?

2 What are some other sources of energy?

3 Are these energy sources common in your country? If not, what sources are common? Why?

4 What are the pros and cons of these sources of energy?

PREPARING TO WATCH

ACTIVATING YOUR
KNOWLEDGE

1 Work with a partner. Discuss the questions.

1 Why do people build wind turbines?
2 Have you ever seen wind turbines? Where? Describe them.

PREDICTING CONTENT
USING VISUALS

2 Work with a partner. Look at the photos from the video. Discuss the questions.

1 How big do you think wind turbines are? Compare them to a building you know.
2 Why would people put a wind turbine in the ocean?
3 Why might a ship have "legs"?

GLOSSARY

run out (phr v) when there is nothing left of something because it has all been used

alternative energy (n phr) power that comes from natural resources like the sun or wind

turbine (n) a type of machine through which air or water flows and turns a special wheel with blades to produce power

assemble (v) to build something by putting parts together

WHILE WATCHING

3 ▶ Watch the video. Write *T* (true), *F* (false), or *DNS* (does not say) next to the statements. Then, correct the false statements.

___T___ 1 People are using wind as a source of energy these days.

_____

___F___ 2 The ship made it possible to build the turbines in the middle of London.

_____in the open sea_____

___T___ 3 The turbines can get energy even from light winds.

_____

___F___ 4 It was difficult to build the turbines in sunny weather.

_____windy_____

___T___ 5 One turbine can provide energy for thousands of homes.

_____

4 ▶ Watch the video again. Complete the sentences with the numbers in the box.

| 12 | 120 | 175 | 3,000 | 500,000 |

1 The wind farm is about __12__ miles from the coast of England.
2 There are __175__ turbines in the London Array.
3 Each of the turbines is about __120__ meters across.
4 Each turbine can provide electricity for __3,000__ homes.
5 The London Array provides electricity to more than __500,000__ homes.

DISCUSSION

5 Work with a partner. Discuss the questions.

1 Do you agree or disagree with the following statement?
The government of my country should build more sources of alternative energy, like wind turbines.
Give reasons and examples for your answer.

2 What could you do in your home to use less energy?

PREPARING TO LISTEN

UNDERSTANDING
KEY VOCABULARY

1 You are going to listen to a lecture. Before you listen, circle the best definition for the word in bold.

1 Fossil fuels are a **limited** source of energy. Some scientists predict that they will be gone by the end of this century.

  a expensive   **c** dirty

  b small in amount or number

2 Wind can **provide** people with energy that is cheap and clean.

  a to give something   **c** to depend on something

  b to make something

3 One **solution** to the problem of climate change is to use public transportation.

  a a result of something   **c** a connection to something

  b a way of solving a problem

4 We should use fewer fossil fuels and more **alternative** forms of energy, such as solar and wind power.

  a cleaner

  b less expensive

  c different from what is usual or traditional

5 Climate change is the world's biggest **environmental** issue. If we don't do something about it, it will have terrible effects on the planet.

  a relating to the weather   **c** important

  b relating to the air, water, and land

6 Scientists have developed a new **system** for growing food. It involves using solar energy to grow food in the desert.

  a an idea   **c** a way of doing things

  b a farm

7 Water is the world's most important **resource**, so it's important to protect it.

  a something you have and can use

  b a kind of energy

  c a body of water, such as a lake or ocean

8 It hasn't rained in six months, so our area is experiencing a water **crisis**.

  a a plan to fix something

  b an organization

  c a very dangerous or difficult situation

2 Work in a group of three. Look at the pictures and answer the questions.

1 What do you think will be the topic of the lecture?

_____

2 What do you think is happening in the pictures?

_____

أكار وتشد

3 What sources of energy are used on this farm?

_____

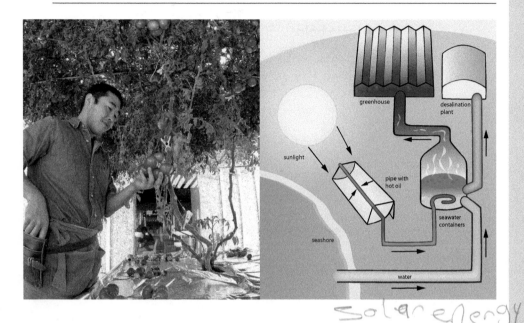

solar energy

PRONUNCIATION FOR LISTENING

SKILLS

Connected speech: linking sounds

When people speak fluently, there is often an extra linking sound between words when the first word ends with a vowel sound and the second word starts with a vowel sound. Common linking sounds are /j/ and /w/.

This type of farming could solve some of the environmental problems we /j/ are now facing.
The rest of the heated water goes to /w/ a desalination plant.

3 ▶ 2.1 Listen to the sentences. What linking sound do you hear between the words in bold? Write *j* or *w* next to each sentence.

PRISM Online Workbook

1 Today I want **to explain** some alternative solutions. _w_
2 As **we all** know, in order to grow plants we need water and sunlight. _j_
3 I think that desert farms might **be a** very interesting way to farm in the future. _j_
4 If **you add** the nutrients to water, you can grow your fruit and vegetables in water. _w_

4 ▶ 2.2 Listen to the lecture and circle the best answers.

1 Desert farming uses solar energy and *water* / *traditional farming*.
2 NASA has been researching hydroponics because it allows us to grow
   food *with more water* / *in extreme climates.*
3 The greenhouse is heated by using *fresh water* / *solar power*.
4 Food from desert farms contains *no pesticides* / *more salt*.
5 Desert farms *use fossil fuels* / *can help solve the global food problem*.

5 ▶ 2.3 Listen again to part of the lecture and complete the summary.

- The farm is only (1) **110** yards or
- (2) **100 meters** meters from the sea.
- Heat is reflected from the (3) **sea** onto a pipe that has oil inside.
- The hot oil heats up the (4) **sea water**.
- When the seawater is at a temperature of (5) **320** °F or (6) **160** °C, the steam heats the greenhouse.
- The desalination plant produces (7) **to 2,700** gallons or (8) **10,000** liters of fresh water every day.
- No pesticides are used during the process.
- This type of farming has a minimal effect on the (9) **enviroment**.

Listening for explanations

In a lecture, speakers often explain difficult or new words. They do this by using certain phrases (e.g., *this means*) or by saying the same word in a simpler way.

Hydroponics means growing plants in water.

6 Match the excerpts from the lecture to the ways of explaining difficult or new words.

LISTENING FOR TEXT
ORGANIZATION

1 Scientists have decided to combine the modern technology of solar energy with a farming technology called hydroponics. **Hydroponics means growing plants in water.** _b_

2 They need nutrients to help them grow. **Nutrients are like food for the plants.** _a_

3 The rest of the heated water goes to a desalination plant. **Desalination is when we remove the salt from seawater to create drinkable water.** _c_

4 Many supermarkets are interested in buying these vegetables because they are grown without pesticides **or other chemicals.** _d_

The lecturer ...

a gives a simple example of what these things are similar to.

b says what group of things this belongs to.

c gives a simple explanation of a process.

d explains what the word means.

DISCUSSION

7 Work in a small group and discuss the questions.

1 Do you know how the food you eat is grown? Is this important to you? Why or why not?

2 Would you mind paying a lot more money for food if you knew it was produced in an environmentally friendly way? Why or why not?

3 What do you think might be some problems with hydroponics?

NEGATIVE PREFIXES

44

PRISM Online Workbook

1 Match the prefixes to the correct words in the chart. Use a dictionary to help you.

advantage	~~caffeinated~~	certain
experienced	regular	social	spell

prefix	meaning	example
un- *social*	not *unhappy*	*uncertain, unusual* *uncomfortable*
in- *perfect*	not *incorrect*	
ir- *regular*	not	
dis- *like*	not	*disadvantage*
de- *activate*	remove / take away	decaffeinated
mis-	wrongly	*misspell*
anti-	against	

ageing.

2 Write the correct prefix to complete the words.

1 Those facts are all ___*in*___correct. Would you like me to give you the right information?

2 Max is an ___*ir*___responsible student. He often forgets to do his homework, and he's usually late to class.

3 Did you ___*mis*___understand the teacher? She said to work in groups, not pairs.

4 I'm definitely ___*anti*___war. I don't think fighting ever solves a country's problems.

5 I ___*dis*___approve of using chemicals to grow food. It's bad for the environment, and it's bad for people's health.

6 Andrea was spending too much time on social media, so she ___*de*___activated all her accounts. But now she doesn't know what's going on in the world.

7 Solar power is cheap, clean, and ___*un*___limited. There will always be enough of it.

MODAL VERBS TO EXPRESS FUTURE POSSIBILITY

45

Use the modal *will* (or *won't*) to say that you are certain about the future.

If there is an accident, then it **will** be huge, and it **will** have long-term effects on the environment.

Use the modals *may*, *might*, and *could* to say that you are uncertain about the future.

We will briefly discuss how this type of farming **could/might/may** solve some of the environmental problems we are now facing.

Might is more common than *may* in conversation. *May* sounds more formal.

PRISM Online Workbook

3 ▶ 2.4 Listen and complete these excerpts from the lecture.

1 Today I want to explain some alternative solutions that ___May___ help reduce some of the problems related to climate change.

2 NASA scientists have been developing this method of growing food because it ___Could___ allow us to grow food in any climate.

3 I think that desert farms ___Might___ be a very interesting way to farm in the future.

4 Write the correct modal verb in the correct place in the sentences. More than one answer may be possible.

1 Farming in the desert solves the problem of food crisis. (uncertainty in the future)
   Farming in the desert **might** solve the problem of food crisis.

2 Not using fossil fuels reduces global warming. (uncertainty in the future)
   _____ might reduce _____

3 Taxing fossil fuels reduces the use of cars. (certainty in the future)
   _____ will reduce _____

4 Using solar energy does not lead to any environmental disasters. (certainty in the future)
   _____ will not lead _____

PREPARING TO LISTEN

UNDERSTANDING KEY VOCABULARY

PRISM Online Workbook

1 You are going to listen to a debate about nuclear power. Before you listen, read the information about wind power. Complete the definitions with the correct form of the words in bold.

Many people think wind power has many **benefits**. First, it is environmentally friendly; it does not **pollute** the environment. Also, unlike coal mines and nuclear power plants, it is unlikely to cause accidents and never leads to **disasters**. Therefore, there is a very low **risk** of danger. Most importantly, this source of energy is **affordable**. However, **opponents** of wind power argue that the wind turbines can have a negative effect on the environment. They say that a turbine takes up a lot of space. Another point is that the wind turbines are not a **long-term** source of energy, unlike nuclear power plants.

1 ___benefits___ (n) advantages
2 ___risk___ (n) the possibility of something bad happening
3 ___long-term___ (adj) continuing for a long time
4 ___disasters___ (n) terrible accidents that cause a lot of damage
5 ___affordable___ (adj) not expensive
6 ___opponents___ (n) people who disagree with an idea
7 ___pollute___ (v) to make something, like air or water, dirty or harmful

odd مهدد

2 Work in a small group. What do you think are the advantages and disadvantages of nuclear power? Write your ideas in the chart.

advantages	disadvantages
It is used to pump water ‹‹ LP	Expensive اغلى
Produce non polluting chemicals كانيوم فيلو	Fear of radiation on human safety
Consume less Fuel	Difficulty disposing of radioactive waste صعوبة التخلص من النفايات - الاشعاعية
Produces large amounts of energy	

3 ▶ 2.5 Listen to the debate about nuclear power. Do the speakers mention any of the ideas that you listed in Exercise 2? Underline them in the chart above.

WHILE LISTENING

**TAKING NOTES ON
MAIN IDEAS**

4 ▶ 2.5 Listen to the debate again. Are Emma and Jack for or against nuclear energy? What are some of the reasons they give? Take notes.

Emma   Jack

For or against: For or against:

Reasons: Reasons:

LISTENING FOR DETAILS

5 ▶ 2.5 Listen to the debate again and circle the correct answer.

1 What are two reasons why Emma mentions the Fukushima nuclear power plant?

  a To say that nuclear power plants can be dangerous.

  b To show that nuclear energy can help develop a country.

  c To give an example of the long-term effects of a nuclear disaster.

  d To show that nuclear power is usually safe.

2 What three arguments are mentioned in favor of nuclear energy?

  a It's cheap.

  b It doesn't pollute the air.

  c It uses advanced technology.

  d It can supply a lot of electricity for a long time.

3 What are two ways that nuclear energy can help developing countries?

  a They can export the energy.

  b They can buy the energy.

  c They can develop new technology.

  d They can be independent of gas and oil prices..

Listening for counterarguments

In a debate or a discussion, speakers often use counterarguments to argue against the opposing viewpoint. Speakers sometimes introduce a counterargument with words or phrases like *despite that* or *however*.

Some people think that nuclear power is an environmentally friendly source of energy because it creates less pollution than traditional power plants. **However**, the opponents of nuclear energy believe that it has more dangers than benefits.

6 Read these excerpts from the debate. What idea is the speaker arguing *against* in each excerpt?

Jack 1 Some people are worried that nuclear power is a big risk. **Despite that**, there are hundreds of nuclear power plants all over the world, and there have only been three major nuclear accidents in the last 30 years.
The speaker is arguing against _the idea that Nuclear is a big risk a big risk_

2 Some people say that nuclear energy doesn't pollute the air, **but that's not completely true**. It takes many years to build a nuclear power plant. During this time, hundreds of machines work day and night and pollute the air in the area.
Emma The speaker is arguing against _the idea that nuclear energy deasn't pollute the air_

DISCUSSION

7 Work in a small group. Use your notes from Listening 1 and Listening 2 to answer the following questions.

1 What are some similarities between hydroponics and nuclear energy? What are some differences?

2 Do you think nuclear power is a good energy solution? Why or why not?

3 What do you think is the best form of energy? Why?

SYNTHESIZING

Power Nuclear

SPEAKING

50 *nuclei* *ann.. gd*

CRITICAL THINKING

At the end of this unit, you are going to do the Speaking Task below.

▎Take part in a debate about building a new shopping mall. You are
a member of a city council. The city council has to decide how to
develop a large piece of land. Some members of the city council want
to build a shopping mall. Argue for or against building a new shopping
mall in your city.

SKILLS

Making counterarguments

Use counterarguments to help make your point stronger. To make an effective
counterargument, first show that you understand the opposing viewpoint.
Some people think that solar and wind energy are greener than
nuclear energy.

Then explain the weaknesses of the opposing viewpoint.
However, I don't think that's accurate. Wind turbines are not exactly
friendly for birds, not to mention that solar panels and wind turbines
take up a lot of space.

▲ UNDERSTAND

1 Complete the chart. Make notes about the opinions of the speakers in
Listening 2. Use your notes from Exercise 4 on page 47 to help you.

	for/against nuclear power	arguments	counterarguments
Emma *against*	① nuclear plants accidents	its true that there are few accident but when it happen it will be huge	it will have long term effects on the enviroment.
Jack *for*	Nuclear Power is most environmentally friendly, and the most sostainable source of energy	some people worried that nuclear power is big risk	+ there are hunderds nuclear power plants all over the world

2 Work in a small group. Think of some of the advantages and disadvantages of building a shopping mall in your town or city. Write your ideas in the chart. Decide whether you are for or against the mall.

advantages of a shopping mall	disadvantages of a shopping mall
1) a lot of new jobs will be 2) helping the city economi 3) There is a place for walk, cinemes and, restauramts 4)	Spending long hoors in the mall 2) very crowded in the week end 3- Always announce discounts always makes expenses

I am *for* / *against* building a shopping mall in our city. people will serd on orc bay on disconts Items,

3 Write your best ideas from Exercise 2 in the *arguments* column (advantages OR disadvantages – not both).

for/against shopping mall	arguments	counterarguments
I am against building a new shopping mall in our city	I am environmenly friendly	

4 Look at your ideas in Exercise 2 that support the opposite viewpoint. Think of what you will say in response to those arguments to make your argument stronger. Write your ideas in the *counterarguments* column in the chart in Exercise 3.

52

LINKING IDEAS WITH TRANSITION WORDS AND PHRASES

Speakers use transition words and phrases to link ideas. Different words and phrases are used for different purposes.

to explain a sequence of ideas	to compare and contrast ideas	to add another idea	to summarize ideas
to begin with	despite that	and	all in all
second	in contrast	also	to sum up
next	although	what's more	overall
finally	but	in addition	in short
	on the other hand	moreover	
	in comparison	not to mention that	

PRISM Online Workbook

1 Circle the correct word or phrase in the sentences.

1 In my opinion, nuclear energy is safe. *Also* / *Although*, it's cheap and clean.

2 Solar energy is an unlimited source of energy. *On the other hand* / *In addition*, it's safe and environmentally friendly.

3 Wind turbines don't destroy the landscape. *Despite that* / *What's more*, they can be dangerous for birds.

4 There are many reasons why we should build a solar power plant. *In addition* / *To begin with*, solar energy is affordable and safe.

5 *First* / *However*, I think that nuclear power plants look ugly and destroy the landscape. *What's more* / *Finally*, they don't always provide jobs for local people.

53

2 Read excerpts from a discussion about building a new nuclear power plant near a city. Complete the excerpts with words and phrases from the box.

addition	begin	comparison	first of all
however	overall	second	the other hand

A: I would like to say that I completely disagree with the idea of building a nuclear power plant so close to the city. To (1)____begin____ with, I understand that modern nuclear power plants are safer than they used to be, and that the plant would be far from our houses. (2)__however__, I worry about my children. If there is a nuclear disaster, our children will be exposed to radiation.

B: I have to agree with this. I worry about the nuclear waste. There are two big questions here. (3)__First of all__, how can we make sure that it doesn't leak into our water supply or soil? (4)__Second__, where are we going to throw away the nuclear waste? I don't think the government should go ahead with this project. Instead, we could build a solar power plant. It would be cleaner. So, (5)__overall__, I think that solar energy would be the best option.

C: I don't think it's completely true that solar panels are better than nuclear energy. Solar power is very expensive to set up, and then what? In (6)__addition__, a nuclear power plant would be cheaper in the long term. And it would create more jobs.

D: I agree that our city needs more jobs. In (7)__comparison__, we need cheap, affordable energy. On the one hand, it's clear that a nuclear power plant will solve both these problems. On (8)__the other hand__, I worry about the plant being so close to our homes. I suggest that we build it as far from the city as possible.

TALKING ABOUT ADVANTAGES AND DISADVANTAGES

3 Look at the excerpts from a debate about solar energy. Do the words/ phrases in bold talk about advantages or disadvantages? Write *A* for advantage or *D* for disadvantage.

1 In my opinion, there are many **pros** of solar energy. __A__

2 Personally, I think that solar energy **has a negative effect on** our wildlife. __D__

3 **The good thing about** solar energy is that it is cheap. __A__

4 The main **benefit** of solar energy is that it is environmentally friendly. __A__

5 There are several **cons** of using solar energy. __D__

6 The second **drawback** of solar energy is that solar farms are unattractive. __D__

4 Complete the sentences with your own ideas.

1 The biggest drawback of nuclear energy is that ...
   it is very expensive

2 There are many benefits of electric cars. For example, ...
   less fuel and cleaner enviroment .

3 There are many pros and cons of using wind power. For instance, ...
   it kills birds but it produces a lot of energy.

4 There are many disadvantages of using gasoline. For example, ...
   Pulluth the air .

GIVING COUNTERARGUMENTS

5 For each argument write a counterargument. Use a word or phrase from the box and then add your ideas.

> despite   however (x2)   that's completely true

1 People often say that nuclear energy is dangerous. _However_ ,
   it is actually very safe. There have been very few nuclear
   power accidents.

2 Some people say that solar power is the best kind of energy. I'm not
   sure _however_ . _the solar panels take alot of_ ,
   space

3 It may be true that fossil fuels have a negative effect on the
   environment. _despite_ that, _fossil fuel gives alot of energy._

4 Electric cars are environmentally friendly. _that's completly true_ ,
   Electric cars do not emit Corbon dioxid or .
   any smoke or exhaust.

SPEAKING TASK

PRISM Online Workbook

Take part in a debate about building a new shopping mall. You are a member of a city council. The city council has to decide how to develop a large piece of land. Some members of the city council want to build a shopping mall. Argue for or against building a new shopping mall in your city.

PREPARE

1 Look at the chart you created in Exercises 3 and 4 in Critical Thinking. Review your notes and add any new information.

50 — 52

2 Use the Task Checklist below to prepare your argument. You can use language like this:

In my opinion, there are many pros/cons …
First of all, I think that …
The main benefit/drawback is …
A second benefit/drawback is …
To sum up, …

3 Prepare some notes about your counterarguments. You can use language like this:

It may be true that …
However, …
Despite that, …

TASK CHECKLIST	✔
Use clear arguments and counterarguments.	
Link ideas effectively with transition words and phrases.	
Explain advantages and disadvantages in a clear way.	
Use modals to express future possibility.	
Use negative prefixes correctly, where appropriate.	

PRACTICE

4 Work in a group of three with people who have the same viewpoint as you. Practice explaining why you are in favor of or against the shopping mall.

5 Think about your arguments. Discuss ways to improve them.

DISCUSS

6 Work in a group of four. Your group should have two people with each viewpoint. Discuss your ideas and together decide whether the city would be better with a new shopping mall.

7 Present your group's decision to the class and explain your reasons.

ON CAMPUS

ACTIVE LEARNING

PREPARING TO LISTEN

students remember less					students remember more
listening to a lecture	reading a textbook	watching a video or demonstration	discussing a topic	doing a task	teaching another student

1 You are going to listen to an interview about active learning. Before you listen, work with a partner and discuss the questions.

    1 According to the diagram above, what is the best way to learn information?

    2 What do you think *active learning* is?

WHILE LISTENING

2 ▶ 2.6 Listen to the interview. Check the activities that Dr. Ferraro mentions.

reading and underlining ☐   doing homework ☐

summarizing ☐   asking questions ☐

watching videos ☐   taking tests ☐

making presentations ☐   project work ☐

3 ▶ 2.6 Circle the best phrases to complete the summary. Then, listen to the interview again to check your answers.

    1 Active learning involves *reading and listening / thinking and talking*.

    2 According to Dr. Ferraro, a good way to read is to *make a summary of the information / underline important points in the textbook*.

    3 An example of transferring material into a different format is *making presentations with visuals / summarizing in your own words*.

    4 Dr. Ferraro's student made presentations for *his class / his study group*.

    5 Asking questions helps students *connect information to their own experience / remember information*.

    6 Compared to more traditional forms of learning, active learning is probably *easier / more difficult*.

4 Work in a small group and discuss the questions.

    1 What examples of active learning have you experienced?

    2 Do you agree that active learning is more effective? Why or why not?

    3 Do you agree that active learning is more difficult? Why or why not?

Active learning strategies

Use active learning strategies to help yourself learn better. You can:

- make summaries, charts, diagrams, and notes to remember information.
- ask questions when you don't understand.
- try to connect the information to your own experience.
- form a study group with other students.

PRACTICE

5 Are you an active learner? Read the statements and check your answers.

	usually or often	sometimes	rarely or never
I make diagrams, charts, and visuals to help myself remember material.			
I write notes and comments on the pages of my textbooks.			
I try to summarize what I have read.			
I come to class with questions for the teacher.			
I ask for help if I need it.			
I often speak up during class.			
I try to make connections to my own experience.			
I often work with other students.			

6 Work with a partner and compare your answers. What are two things that you could do to help yourself learn better?

REAL-WORLD APPLICATION

7 Work in a small group. You are organizing a workshop for other students on active learning strategies for studying English. Using the principles of active learning, brainstorm one strategy to help yourself learn ...

1 grammar.   3 listening skills.   5 reading skills.
2 vocabulary.   4 speaking skills.   6 writing skills.

8 Work with another group. Compare your strategies. Make a list of the six best strategies. Include examples of each strategy.

9 Present your strategies to the class.

LEARNING OBJECTIVES

Listening skill	Identify rhetorical questions
Pronunciation	Word stress
Speaking skills	Give recommendations; expand on an idea
Speaking Task	Take part in a discussion about a transportation problem
On Campus	Set SMART goals

TRANSPORTATION

59

ACTIVATE YOUR KNOWLEDGE

Work with a partner. Discuss the questions.

1 What are some problems with modern forms of transportation?
2 How has transportation changed in the last 50 years?
3 What do you think is the future of transportation? How will it be different in 50 years?

PREPARING TO WATCH

ACTIVATING YOUR KNOWLEDGE

1 Work with a partner. Discuss the questions.

1 What two places in the world would you like to visit? How long would it take to fly there? How much would it cost?

2 How did people travel between continents before there were airplanes?

PREDICTING CONTENT USING VISUALS

2 Work with a partner. Look at the photos from the video and discuss the questions.

1 When you think about how far apart two places are, do you think of the distance in miles or kilometers, or in minutes or hours?

2 What city could the plane be flying over in the first two photos?

3 How has air travel changed the way that we think about our world?

> **GLOSSARY**
>
> **in no time** (idm) very quickly
>
> **revolutionize** (v) to change something completely so that it is much better than before
>
> **commercial plane** (n phr) a plane that carries passengers or goods; not a military or private plane
>
> **airspace** (n) the air or sky above a place

ships

61

WHILE WATCHING

3 ▶ Watch the video. Complete the paragraph with the words in the box.

busiest business closer commercial larger smaller

In the past 50 years, we've made the world (1) _Smaller_ . Cities and continents are (2) _Closer_ than ever before. Many (3) _business_ people travel great distances every week. Some (4) _Commerc_ planes are bigger than houses. The airspace above London is one of the (5) _busiest_ in the world. The number of people traveling by plane grows (6) _Larger_ every year.

4 ▶ Watch the video again. Circle the words that you hear.

1 Today we can travel from continent to continent *in time* / *in no time.*
2 South America and *Africa* / *Asia* are less than a day away from each other.
3 Military planes travel faster than the speed *of sound* / *light.*
4 Every day *350* / *3,500* flights take place.
5 In *2015* / *2016*, about 3.7 billion people traveled by plane.
6 Right now, around the world, *over* / *under* a million people are traveling in the air.

DISCUSSION

5 Work in a small group. Take turns discussing the questions. Give reasons and examples for your answers.

1 Which do you think has changed the world more: the car or the airplane?
2 How would you describe the average airline customer in your country?
3 How do you think air travel has changed international business?

About Qatar

LISTENING

LISTENING 1

PRONUNCIATION FOR LISTENING

SKILLS

Word stress

Some words have the same form whether they are a noun or a verb.

In recent years, there has been a significant **decrease** in the number of plane crashes. (*decrease* = noun)
To **decrease** the fear of flying, you should avoid watching movies about plane crashes or other accidents. (*decrease* = verb)

However, the pronunciation may not be the same. In many two-syllable words, nouns are stressed on the first syllable and verbs on the second syllable.

de̲crease (= noun)   de̲crease (= verb)

Note that not all words follow this pattern.
co̲ntrol (= noun)   co̲ntrol (= verb)

PRISM Online Workbook

1 ▶ 3.1 Listen to the two sentences and answer the questions.

1 There has been an **increase** in motorcycle accidents over the past five years.

2 Airlines are always looking for new ways to **increase** the safety of their planes.

a In which sentence is *increase* a verb? in ___
b In which sentence is *increase* a noun? in ___
c Where is the stress in each word?
   Verb: _____   Noun: _____

2 ▶ 3.2 Listen and circle the stressed syllable in the words in bold.

1 There's a detailed **record** of each plane crash.
2 A machine called a "black box" **records** everything that the pilot and copilot say during a flight.
3 Some cities don't **permit** biking on the sidewalk.
4 I'm sorry, but you need an employee parking **permit** to park in this garage.
5 The company **presents** an award for road safety to the safest city.
6 He received a new car as a birthday **present**.

3 Practice saying the sentences in Exercise 2.

PREPARING TO LISTEN

63

4 You are going to listen to a radio program about the fear of flying. Before you listen, read the definitions. Complete the sentences with the correct form of the words in bold.

> **avoid** (v) to stay away from something
> **compare** (v) to look for the difference between two or more things
> **consist of** (v) to be made of something
> **crash** (n) an accident in which a vehicle hits something
> **cure** (n) something that will make a sick person healthy again
> **extreme** (adj) very large in amount or degree
> **safety** (n) the condition of not being in danger
> **scared** (adj) feeling fear or worry

1 When there are _extreme_ weather conditions, such as a big snowstorm or a hurricane, airports sometimes close.
2 Before you book a flight, be sure to _compare_ prices from different airlines to get the best deal.
3 There was a five-car _crash_ on the highway this morning. Fortunately, everyone survived.
4 I try to _avoid_ driving to work because traffic is terrible. I usually take the subway instead.
5 There isn't a _cure_ for the common cold, but washing your hands often can help to protect you from colds.
6 The word *aerophobia* comes from the Greek, and it _consist of_ two parts: *aero*, which means "flight" or "air," and *phobia*, which means "fear."
7 If you're _scared_ of flying, you're not alone. About 25% of people have a fear of flying.
8 _safety_ is very important to airlines. They inspect their planes before every flight.

USING YOUR
KNOWLEDGE

5 Work in a small group and discuss the questions.

1 Do you enjoy flying? Why or why not? *No*
2 Have you ever had a scary experience on a flight? What happened?
3 Which of these forms of transportation do you think is the most dangerous? Which do you think is the safest? Why? *risk*

a flying
b traveling by car

c traveling by motorcycle
d walking

I walk on the ground

WHILE LISTENING

LISTENING FOR
MAIN IDEAS

6 ▶ 3.3 Listen to the first part of a radio program and circle the correct answer.

1 What is the main idea of the program?
  a the history of airplanes
  b the fear of flying and how to reduce it
  c plane crash investigations

2 What did Mark use to be?
  a He was a flight attendant.
  b He was a psychologist.
  c He was a pilot.

3 What did Mark do to help himself?
  a He searched for advice on the Internet.
  b He talked to his friends.
  c He studied air safety.

4 Can a fear of flying be cured?
  a Yes, but not always.
  b Anyone can get rid of the fear of flying.
  c No, it can't.

TAKING NOTES
ON DETAILS

7 ▶ 3.4 Listen to the second part of the radio program. Complete the notes using the words in the box.

avoid	damaged	driving	engines	flying	normal	reduce	wings

Many steps you can take to (1) reduce the fear of flying:
- Learn how a plane works – helps you understand planes can fly without the (2) engines because the (3) wings push against the air + keep plane flying
- Turbulence is (4) normal and can only cause an accident if plane is already (5) damaged
- Learn where things are on a plane
- (6) avoid disaster movies
- Be realistic – remember (7) flying is much safer than (8) driving

8 Work with a partner. Read the list of tips on how to deal with and control a fear of flying. How useful do you think each tip is? Discuss your ideas.

1 Learn how airplanes work. ☐ *No*
2 Imagine you are on a bus or train. ☐ *No*
3 Take something to help you sleep on the plane. ☑
4 Learn the layout of the plane before takeoff. ☑
5 Go to a psychologist. ☐ *No*
6 Don't watch movies or TV shows about air disasters. ☑

9 ▶ 3.4 Listen to the second part of the radio program again and check the tips in Exercise 8 that Mark mentions.

LISTENING FOR DETAILS

POST-LISTENING

SKILLS

Rhetorical questions

Rhetorical questions are not the same as real questions. They are used to bring the listener's attention to a topic or an idea. The speaker does not expect an answer to the question.

When you ask **regular questions**, you stop speaking and wait for an answer.

When you ask **rhetorical questions**, you continue speaking.

10 ▶ 3.3 Listen to the first part of the radio program again. Which questions are rhetorical questions? Which are real questions? Check your answers.

LISTENING FOR TEXT ORGANIZATION

PRISM Online Workbook

	real	rhetorical
1 Have you ever been afraid of flying?	☐	☑
2 Do you feel scared when you sit on a plane?	☐	☑
3 Are you stressed when there's turbulence?	☑	☑
4 Can you tell us more about your experience, Mark?	☑	☐
5 Did it make you afraid of flying?	☑	☐
6 What was I supposed to do?	☐	☑
7 Can it be cured?	☐	☑

DISCUSSION

11 Work in a small group. A phobia is an extreme fear of something. Look at the phobias and discuss the questions.

- *arachnophobia* – fear of spiders
- *trypanophobia* – fear of needles
- *ailurophobia* – fear of cats
- *aquaphobia* – fear of water
- *claustrophobia* – fear of being in a closed space
- *nomophobia* – fear of being outside of a cell phone network
- *cynophobia* – fear of dogs
- *acrophobia* – fear of heights

1 Do you know anyone with a phobia? What phobia does the person have?
2 What do you think are the most common phobias?
3 What do you think are the most common causes of phobias?
4 Do you think it's possible to cure a phobia? If yes, how?

⊙ LANGUAGE DEVELOPMENT

TALKING ABOUT PROBLEMS AND SOLUTIONS

1 Read the sentences. Circle the correct definition for the words and phrases in bold.

1 I read stories of people who managed to **control** their fear of flying.
   a to remove something
   b to limit the number or amount of something
   c to understand something

2 For someone who has to travel for work, aerophobia is a **serious** problem.
   a important; bad
   b funny
   c unusual

3 To help **solve** its traffic problems, the city is building a new highway.
   a to understand something
   b to learn something
   c to find a way to fix a problem

4 Most turbulence is normal and won't cause any **trouble**, so you shouldn't be scared of it.
   a accidents
   b fear
   c problems

5 The course had a strong **impact** on me. I actually became very scared of being on a plane.
   a effect
   b difference
   c stress

6 There are several ways to reduce your fear of flying. The first **method** is to learn more about how planes work.
   a way of doing something
   b idea about something
   c answer to something

7 The engine is broken. The mechanics are trying to **figure out** how to fix it.
   a to research a problem
   b to think about a problem until you know the answer
   c to use math to find the answer to a problem

8 How did it **influence** you? Did it make you afraid of flying?
   a to affect how someone acts or thinks
   b to scare someone
   c to teach someone

2 Work with a partner. Discuss the questions.

1 What problems does your city have with transportation?
2 Think of a problem that you have had in your life. How did you solve it?
3 Think of a challenge you might face in the future. What do you need to figure out to solve it?

COMPARATIVE AND SUPERLATIVE ADJECTIVES

Comparative adjectives say how two things or ideas are different.

subject	verb	comparative adjective	*than*	object
Taking a train		greener		driving.
Flying	is	scarier	than	taking a train.
Driving		more affordable		flying.

Superlative adjectives describe how a person or a thing is different from all others.

subject	verb	*the*	superlative adjective	object
Walking			greenest	
Flying	is	the	scariest	form of transportation.
Taking a bus			most affordable	

PRISM Online Workbook

3 ▶ 3.5 Listen to the sentences. Circle the syllable that has the most stress in each phrase in bold.

1 The course was a **lot more challenging than** I expected.
2 We can see that **by far the most affordable form of transportation** is walking.
3 The risks of driving a car are **considerably more significant than** those of flying.
4 For me, flying is **much more comfortable than** traveling by train.
5 Taking a train is **definitely more relaxing than** driving.

4 Answer the questions.

1 Which sentences in Exercise 3 use the comparative form? _3, 4, 5_
2 Which sentences use the superlative form? _2_
3 Which words or phrases are used to emphasize the comparatives? Underline them.
4 What is the meaning of the words or phrases you underlined?
_____

5 Complete the sentences with the correct form of the adjectives in parentheses.

1 When I drive, I prefer to take _more direct_ route rather than the fastest route, because it saves gas. (direct)
2 I'm always _calmer_ in a car than in a plane. (calm)
3 Using cell phones while driving is the _most serious_ driving safety issue. (serious)
4 Driving your own car is the _most comfortable_ way to travel. (comfortable)
5 If you are in a hurry, it is _faster_ to ride a bike than to drive a car. (fast)
6 Buying a monthly pass for public transportation is _more affordable_ than paying for every ride. (affordable)
7 The _most appropriate_ tip for a taxi driver is 20% of the fare. (appropriate)

PREPARING TO LISTEN

UNDERSTANDING KEY VOCABULARY

PRISM Online Workbook

1 You are going to listen to a presentation about biking to work. Before you listen, complete the definitions with the correct form of the words in bold.

c 1 Did you **injure** your knee when you fell off your bike?

d 2 Drivers should always have **respect** for pedestrians and stop for them.

f 3 I got a **fine** for driving through a red light. It was over $50.

h 4 Some teenagers **break the law** by driving without a license.

g 5 We can **prevent** accidents by driving within the speed limit.

b 6 Many accidents happen when drivers **pass** other cars without checking their mirrors.

a 7 Many people drive cars to work because it's more **convenient** to sit comfortably in your own vehicle.

e 8 Our city has a lot of traffic problems. To **solve** some of them, we're encouraging people to bike more and drive less.

a ~~Convenient~~ (adj) easy to use or suiting your plans well

b _pass_ (v) to go past someone or something

c _injure_ (v) to hurt or cause physical harm

d _respect_ (n) polite behavior towards someone

e _solve_ (v) to find a way to fix a problem

f _fine_ (n) money that has to be paid as a punishment for not obeying a law

g _prevent_ (v) to stop something from happening

h _break the law_ (v) to fail to obey the rules of a country, state or city

USING YOUR KNOWLEDGE

2 Work with a partner and discuss the questions.

1 What are some of the reasons that people bike in a big city? *cheaper*

2 What are some advantages of biking to work? *No parking problem*

3 What are some problems with biking to work? *weather Ring*

WHILE LISTENING

3 ▶ 3.6 Listen to the first part of the presentation and answer the
questions.

if

1 What is the goal of the Wheels to Work organization?

_____ *if wheels to* _____

2 What three main issues with biking to work does the speaker mention?

a *some people riding bike to work isn't convenient*

b *they sometimes work late and don't wont to bike home in the dark*

c *alot of people don't like home in the rain*

4 ▶ 3.6 Listen to the first part of the presentation again. Check the
problems that the speaker mentions.

1 Most people don't have bikes. ☑
2 There's a lot of traffic. ☑
3 There aren't any bike lanes. ☒
4 The bike lanes are too narrow. ☑
5 Cars sometimes drive in the bike lanes. ☒
6 There's nowhere to put your bike while you're working. ☒
7 It's too cold. ☒
8 There's nowhere to shower at work. ☒
9 Some people live far away from work. ☑
10 People don't want to ride their bikes at night. ☑

5 ▶ 3.7 Listen to the second part of the presentation.
What recommendations does the speaker make? What would
be the results of the recommendations? Take notes.

recommendations	possible results
1	First
2	
3	
4	
5	

POST-LISTENING

6 ▶ 3.7 Listen to the second part of the presentation again. Check the expressions that are used to introduce recommendations.

1 I'd suggest that ... ☒ Police-
2 I think it would be much better if ... ☐ oil
3 I'd like to see ... ☒ wider
4 I think it would be safer if ... ☐
5 We should ... ☒ also
6 I'd like it if ... ☒
7 (They) ought to ... ☑
8 In my opinion, we should ... ☒
9 The best thing would be if ... ☐

7 Work with a partner. What could be done to improve your town or city? Take turns proposing ideas. Use some of the expressions in Exercise 6.

DISCUSSION

8 Work in a small group. Think about Listenings 1 and 2 and answer the questions.

1 Flying is much safer than biking, yet most people have a greater fear of flying than of biking. What do you think are the reasons for this?
2 Do you think the ideas from Listening 2 would work to encourage more biking in your town or city? If not, what ideas would work? Why?

CRITICAL THINKING

73.

At the end of this unit, you are going to do the Speaking Task below.

> Give a presentation on a transportation problem and suggest solutions to solve the problem.

1 Complete the chart with the problems, proposed solutions, and predicted results from Listening 2. Use information from your notes on page 72.

UNDERSTAND ▲

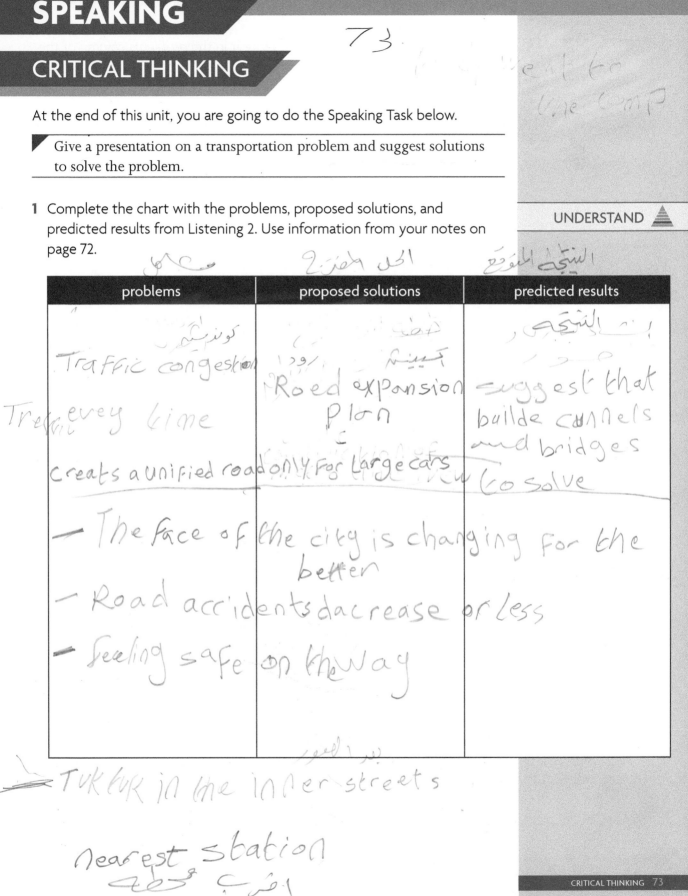

problems	proposed solutions	predicted results
Traffic congeskon	Road expansion plan	suggest that builde cunnels and bridges to solve
Trefic evey time		
creats a unified road only for large cars		
— The face of the city is changing for the better		
— Road accidents dacrease or less		
— feeling safe on the way		

Tuk tuk in the inner streets

nearest station

7 4

REMEMBER

APPLY

2 Work with a partner. Think about the transportation problems in your city or country. Write a list of the problems.

3 Choose a transportation problem. Write it in the *problems* column of the presentation planning chart below. What are some possible solutions to the problem? Write them in the *proposed solutions* column.

problems	proposed solutions	predicted results

ANALYZE

4 What do you predict the results would be of each solution? Write your ideas in the *predicted results* column above. Which solution do you think is best? Circle it.

PREPARATION FOR SPEAKING

GIVING RECOMMENDATIONS   75

SKILLS

Speakers use certain phrases to give recommendations, that is, ideas about what they think should be done. Here are some phrases you can use to give recommendations:

In my opinion, we should ...
I'd like it if ...
We ought to ...
I think it would be better if ...
The best thing would be if ...
I'd like to see ...
I'd suggest that ...
I (don't) think ...

I'd like it if we had wider bike lanes.
I think it would be better if / The best thing would be if garages had an area to park bikes.
I'd like to see bike racks on buses.
I'd suggest that we put bike racks on buses.

1 ▶ 3.8 Listen to a group discussion about the problem of eating while driving. Who do you agree with most? _____

PRISM Online Workbook

2 Look at the excerpts. Underline the phrases that introduce a recommendation or proposal.

   1 <u>I don't think</u> the government should do anything about it.
   2 I think it would be better if they closed drive-through restaurants.
   3 I think it would be much better if drivers weren't allowed to eat or drink while they drive.
   4 The best thing would be to have more cameras on the roads to record what drivers are doing.
   5 I'd suggest that the police give the drivers points on their license.

EXPANDING ON AN IDEA

SKILLS

When speakers propose an idea or make a recommendation, they often state the idea first and then give more details about it. Details can include reasons and examples from personal experience.

Idea: I think it would be better if they closed drive-through restaurants.

Reason: This is because they only encourage drivers to buy food and eat it while they drive.

Example from personal experience: Last week, I bought some coffee and something to eat on the way to work ...

PRISM **Online** Workbook

3 The speakers in the group discussion expand on their ideas. Match the details to the ideas in Exercise 2. There is one extra idea.

a <u>From my own experience</u>, I can tell you that it can be very dangerous. _2_

b <u>Personally</u>, I eat fast food in my car a few times a week and I've never had an accident. _4_

c <u>The reason for this is</u> the police can check the videos to see who's eating, who's texting, and so on. _by_

d <u>This is because</u> they only encourage drivers to buy food and eat it while they drive. _2_

4 Work with a partner. What is your opinion of eating while driving? Discuss your opinion. Give recommendations and examples from personal experience or knowledge.

SPEAKING TASK

Give a presentation on a transportation problem and suggest solutions to solve the problem.

PRISM Online Workbook

PREPARE

1 Look at the chart you created in Exercises 3 and 4 in Critical Thinking. Review your notes and add any new information.

2 Use the Task Checklist below to prepare your argument. You can use language like this:

I'd suggest ...

I think it would be better if ...

In my opinion, we should ...

The best thing would be if ...

I'd like to see ...

3 For each proposed solution, make notes about how you will expand on your idea with reasons and examples from personal experience or knowledge. You can use language like this:

The reason for this is ...

This is because ...

From my own experience ...

Personally, ...

TASK CHECKLIST	✔
Compare different options.	
Propose ideas clearly.	
Expand on ideas by giving reasons.	
Talk about personal experiences clearly.	

PRACTICE

4 Work in a small group. Take turns practicing your presentations. Take notes during the discussion. Use your notes to give feedback to each other to improve your presentations.

PRESENT

5 Take turns giving your presentation to the class.

SETTING SMART GOALS

PREPARING TO LISTEN

1 You are going to listen to a lecture about SMART goals. Before you listen, look at the list of goals. Circle three goals that you have.

> be a better student   eat better food   get a good job
> get good grades   get more exercise   graduate on time
> have more free time   help my family   learn a new skill
> speak English well   transfer to a four-year college

2 Work with a partner and compare your goals. Discuss the questions.

  1 Why is each goal important to you?

  2 What other goals do you have?

3 Work with a partner. Look at the words below and discuss the questions.

  1 What does each word mean?

  2 How might each word apply to goal-setting?

> specific   measurable   achievable   relevant   time-bound

WHILE LISTENING

4 ▶ 3.9 Listen to the lecture and complete the notes.

	SMART goals
specific	Identify ⁽¹⁾_____. e.g., What is a good job?
measurable	How will you ⁽²⁾_____?
	e.g., how many hours in the gym, how much ⁽³⁾_____?
achievable	e.g., not "A in all classes" but ⁽⁴⁾_____ = more realistic.
	Ask yourself, ⁽⁵⁾_____? What steps do I need to take?
relevant	Relevant = linked to ⁽⁶⁾_____ objectives
	Ask yourself, "how important in long term?"
time-bound	Decide on a ⁽⁷⁾_____.
	What will you do this week/ next week, etc.?

5 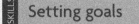 3.9 Listen to the lecture again and check your notes. Then, compare your notes with a partner.

SKILLS

Setting goals

Set goals to help yourself succeed in college. Follow the SMART criteria.

Make your goals:

- specific
- measurable
- achievable
- relevant
- time-bound

PRACTICE

6 Read the questions and write one of the SMART criteria next to each one.

1 How are you going to do this? _____*achievable*_____
2 How many classes are you going to take? _____
3 What is your timeline? _____
4 What steps do you need to take? _____
5 Is this goal important for your future plans? _____
6 What exactly are you going to do? _____
7 When are you going to start? _____
8 How much money do you need to earn? _____

REAL-WORLD APPLICATION

7 Work with a partner. Look at three goals that you identified in Exercises 1 and 2. What questions could you ask to make each goal a SMART goal?

Goal 1: _____

_____

Goal 2: _____

_____

Goal 3: _____

_____

8 Choose one of your goals. Take turns role-playing a conversation with an advisor. Ask the questions to make each goal a SMART goal.

A: I'm going to spend more time on my studies.
B: How much time are you going to spend?
A: I'd like to study about four more hours a week.
B: How are you going to do that?
A: I'm going to study in the library at school.

Listening skills	Identify cause and effect; listen for opinion
Pronunciation	Connected speech: /t/ and /d/ at the end of words; stress patterns in phrases for agreeing and disagreeing
Speaking skills	Be polite in a discussion; use adverbs for emphasis
Speaking Task	Take part in a discussion
On Campus	Deal with culture shock

ACTIVATE YOUR KNOWLEDGE

Popular Places

high - spicelp

Work in a small group. Discuss the questions.

1 Look at the photo. What country do you think it is from? →
   What is the tradition?

2 Do you have any similar traditions in your country? *National day*

3 Do you follow all of your country's traditional customs?
   Why or why not?

PREPARING TO WATCH

ACTIVATING YOUR KNOWLEDGE

1 Work with a partner. Discuss the questions.

1 What are some traditional dances in your country?
2 What kind of dances are popular with young people nowadays?
3 If you go dancing, do you prefer to dance on your own, with a partner, or with a group of friends? Why?

PREDICTING CONTENT USING VISUALS

2 Work with a partner. Look at the photos from the video and discuss the questions.

1 What country do you think the people live in?
2 Are most of these people the same age or different ages?
3 Why do you think the men are wearing black hats?

> **GLOSSARY**
>
> **handkerchief** (n) a square piece of cloth that you use to dry your face or nose
>
> **courtship** (n) the period of time when people have a romantic relationship that often leads to marriage
>
> **rooster** (n) a male chicken
>
> **symbol** (n) a sign or object that is used to represent something

WHILE WATCHING

UNDERSTANDING MAIN IDEAS

3 ▶ Watch the video. Circle the correct answer.

1 The *cueca brava* is a _____ dance.
  a country   **b** national   c city
2 People dance the cueca brava to celebrate National Day in _____ .
  a Mexico   b Colombia   **c** Chile
3 The musicians are playing the accordion, the tambourine, and the _____ .
  a guitar   b piano   c violin

4 Traditionally, a man and a woman hold a _____ in the air while they dance the cueca brava.
  (a) handkerchief   **b** hat   **c** bird

5 Some of the men wear traditional _____ hats.
  a white   **b** red   **(c)** black

4 ▶ Watch the video again. Write _T_ (true) or _F_ (false) next to the statements. Then, correct the false statements.

_F_ 1 The cueca is especially popular in the cities.
_____

_F_ 2 The singer is a writer and movie actor.
_____

_F_ 3 Traditionally, two men face each other and then begin to dance.
_____and women_____

_T_ 4 The dance takes the form of a complex courtship between a rooster and his bird.
_____

_F_ 5 The dance is enjoyed by both teenage and older generations.
_____

DISCUSSION

5 Work in a small group. If possible, work with classmates from different countries or regions. Complete the chart. Then, share your answers with another group.

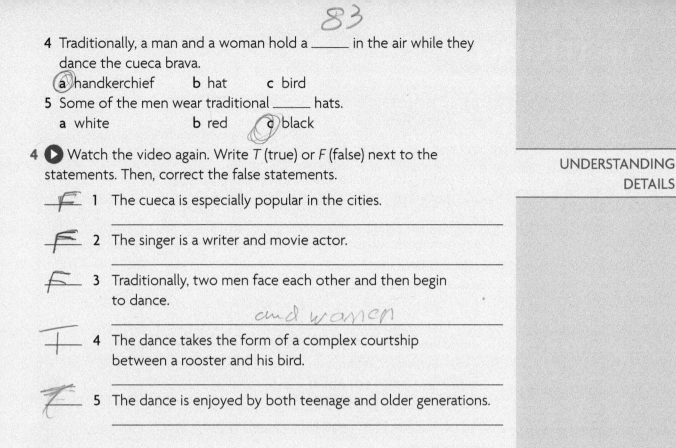

country	dance	reason	people	music	clothes
Chile	cueca brava	to celebrate the nation	everyone	cueca	black hats, handkerchiefs
Egypt	Tredikion Pheronic dance	spring season	Everyone	mostly soprano and oprah	Traditional pheronic costums

LISTENING

PREPARING TO LISTEN

UNDERSTANDING KEY VOCABULARY

1 You are going to listen to a radio program about customs in the modern world. Before you listen circle the correct definitions for the words in bold.

1 My neighborhood is very **multicultural**. People of many cultures and religions live here.

   a busy and crowded

   b including people who have many different customs and beliefs

2 The tradition of letter writing has almost **died out**. These days, everyone communicates by social media, texting, or email.

   a to become more rare and eventually disappear

   b to change into something else

3 Min-Soo **interacts** with a lot of people all day at work, so when he gets home, he likes to relax and spend some time alone.

   a to avoid

   b to communicate and do things with someone/something

4 Tomorrow is my parent's 25th wedding **anniversary**. They're going to have dinner together at a nice restaurant.

   a a party with a lot of guests

   b the day on which an important event happened on a previous year

5 In the United States, most families have a **celebration** on Thanksgiving. They get together with family and friends to enjoy a big meal.

   a a trip to another country

   b an occasion when you do something to mark a special day or event

6 A few **generations** ago, people listened to the radio at night instead of watching TV or going online.

   a all the people of about the same age within a society or a family

   b periods of a few months

7 Anna has had an active **political** career. She was a state representative for several years, and then she became governor.

   a relating to a person's job

   b relating to the activities of the government

8 **Social** anthropologists study the ways in which people live in groups around the world.

   a relating to a large group of people who live together in an organized way

   b relating to countries

2 Work with a partner. Discuss the questions.

85

USING YOUR
KNOWLEDGE

1 What does *tradition* mean? What are the most important customs and traditions in your country or your family? Why are they important?

2 What are some ways that technology has changed people's daily lives in the past 25 years? Do you think these changes are positive or negative?

WHILE LISTENING

LISTENING FOR
MAIN IDEAS

3 ▶ 4.1 Listen to an advertisement for a radio program. Answer the questions.

1 Who is Kevin Lee?

a well-known anthropologist and the author of changing

2 What is the program about?

Book of the week

3 When can you listen to this program?

Sunday 1 PM

4 ▶ 4.2 Listen to the radio program. Which picture shows a tradition that the speaker doesn't mention? *A*

5 ▶ 4.2 Listen to the radio program again. Write notes in the chart.

Effects of modern technology on traditions

	old tradition	new tradition
sending cards or messages	people sent cards	people send messages by email
preparing holiday food	spend alot times effort	buying ready food or going to restorants
recipes	cook Books	internet
where people eat holiday meals	home	restaurants

87

because

Identifying cause and effect

السبب والتأثير

During a lecture or presentation, a speaker sometimes talks about causes. To introduce causes, a speaker can use phrases like: *Due to …* , *The reason for this is …* , *because …* , etc.

Due to modern kitchens, (cause) people don't have to spend much time cooking anymore. (effect)

People don't have to spend much time cooking anymore. (effect) The reason for this is (that) we have modern kitchens. (cause)

The speaker can also introduce **effects**, using phrases like *That's why …* , *This means …* , etc.

As a child, I lived in Japan, Thailand, and Egypt. (cause) That's why I decided to study anthropology. (effect)

You can find any recipe you want on the Internet. (cause) This means that many people don't need cookbooks anymore. (effect)

6 ▶ 4.3 Listen and complete the excerpts from the program.

1 Anthropology, in a general sense, is the study of humanity. I know that's not very exact. *That's why* we have many types of anthropology, like linguistic anthropology and social anthropology.

2 Some traditions die out *because* our way of life changes.

3 Now, *Due to* developments in technology, people spend more time interacting with other people over the Internet.

4 But now we don't have to work so hard. *This is* we have modern kitchens and supermarket food.
because

5 In the United States, on Thanksgiving, which is one of the biggest celebrations, many families go to restaurants *because* they don't want to spend their holiday working in the kitchen.

7 Work with a partner. Underline the cause and circle the effect in each sentence in Exercise 6.

8 Circle the best word or phrase to complete each sentence.

1 *Because* / ~~This means that~~ people spend more time online, our social lives have changed.

2 Both of my parents work full-time. *That's why* / ~~The reason for this is~~ they don't have much time to cook at home.

3 We have developed new technology. ~~Due to~~ / *This means that* our habits have changed.

4 People don't buy many CDs anymore *because* / ~~that's why~~ you can buy digital music.

5 ~~The reason for this is~~ / *Because* of social networking sites, people communicate more over the Internet.

Connected speech: /t/ and /d/ at the end of words

When people speak quickly and naturally, the gaps between words are often not easy to hear, and people don't always pronounce all the letters in a word. For example, they don't always pronounce the /t/ or /d/ sounds at the end of words if they are part of a cluster of consonants.

Listen to this sentence. The letters highlighted in green are not pronounced clearly. The letter highlighted in yellow is pronounced clearly.

▶ 4.4 I study different cultures around the world and how social and political changes affect these cultures.

PRISM Online Workbook

9 ▶ 4.5 Listen to excerpts from the program. Circle the /t/ and /d/ sounds that you can hear clearly in the bold words. In one sentence you don't need to circle any sounds.

1 My book is **about** the **effect** of modern technology on traditions **around** the world.
2 People **spent** a **lot** of time **and effort** preparing special meals.
3 Growing up in **different** cultures helps you realize **that** customs and traditions are often local.
4 We still **spend** time interacting with other people, **but** it's **not** always face-to-face.
5 In the **past**, people **sent** each other cards to celebrate **important** events like birthdays and anniversaries.
6 Traditions **don't** always die out – **but** customs and traditions do change **and adapt** to the modern world.

DISCUSSION

10 Work in a small group. Discuss the questions.

1 Think about the important traditions in your country. Are they still relevant today? Why or why not?
2 Do you know any traditions that have disappeared since your grandparents were young? Why do you think they disappeared?
3 What are some traditions or customs that have changed over the last 20 years? Why have they changed?

SUFFIXES اللوا حق

LANGUAGE

A suffix is a group of letters added to the end of a word to make a new word. Learning the meaning of suffixes is a quick way to expand your vocabulary. Look at how some common suffixes change the meaning of a word.

word	suffix	new word	part of speech	meaning of suffix
tradition	-al	traditional	adjective	relating to
end	-less	endless	adjective	without
accept	-able*	acceptable	adjective	can be
modern	-ize	modernize	verb	cause/become
strength	-en	strengthen	verb	makes the word a verb
develop	-ment	development	noun	action, result
prevent	-ion	prevention	noun	action, process
help	-ful	helpful	adjective	full of

* If the word ends in *y*, change the *y* to *i* and add *able*: deny → deniable

PRISM Online Workbook

1 Correct the mistakes in bold using the word forms in parentheses.

1 Chinese New Year is a great **celebrate**. (noun)
_____ Celebration _____

2 I got 60% on my exam. That's **accept** but not great. (adjective)
_____ acceptable _____

3 I'm in **agree** with you. Your argument really makes sense. (noun)
_____ agreement _____

4 The **politics** situation in this country is very stable. (adjective)
_____ Political _____

5 Public speaking **frights** (verb) many people. It's one of the most common fears.
_____ frightens _____

6 I want to **special** in foreign languages. (verb)
_____ specialize _____

90

2 Complete the sentences with the correct form of the words in parentheses.

1 A lot of people think that it's bad for teenagers to spend so much time on social networking sites, but I think it's _harmful_ (harm). It's just fun!

2 You can find a lot of good, _useful_ (use) information on the Internet. But to be honest, a lot of it is not _reliable_ (rely). You need to be _careful_ (care) about your sources.

3 It's _enjoyable_ (enjoy) to celebrate national holidays.

4 Some people might think you're not _thoughtful_ (thought) if you don't remember their birthday.

3 Work with a partner. Discuss the sentences in Exercise 2. Do you agree or disagree with each sentence? Why?

DEPENDENT PREPOSITIONS

LANGUAGE

Many verbs and adjectives are followed by specific prepositions. These are called "dependent prepositions." It is important to remember these prepositions when you learn a new word. For example, *adapt* means to "become familiar with a new situation":

Customs and traditions do change and <u>adapt to</u> the modern world.

Common verb + preposition combinations

belong to	look at	talk to
laugh at	talk about	worry about

Common adjective + preposition combinations

bad for	full of	surprised by
excited about	responsible for	wrong with

PRISM Online Workbook

4 Circle the correct prepositions. Use a dictionary to help you.

1 Do you adapt quickly *for* / *to* new situations?

2 Do you like listening *for* / *to* traditional music?

3 When you search *for* / *about* information online, what websites do you use most often?

4 Do we always benefit *from* / *about* new technology?

5 Do you worry *about* / *to* spending too much time online?

5 Work with a partner. Ask and answer the questions in Exercise 4.

6 Complete the sentences with a preposition from the box.

> about   by   for (x2)   in   to

1 When did you first become interested ___in___ anthropology?
2 Due ___to___ developments in technology, people communicate less face-to-face.
3 There are people who complain ___about___ the changes that technology has brought to our lives.
4 Looking at a screen for too long can be bad ___for___ your eyes.
5 I was surprised ___by___ the differences between people of different cultures.
6 My grandmother was responsible ___for___ making huge meals for our family celebrations.

LISTENING 2

PREPARING TO LISTEN

UNDERSTANDING
KEY VOCABULARY

PRISM Online Workbook

1 You are going to listen to a discussion about gift giving. Before you listen, read the definitions. Complete the sentences with the correct form of the words in bold.

> **behavior** (n) a particular way of acting
> **commercial** (adj) related to buying and selling things
> **event** (n) anything that happens, especially something important or unusual
> **graduate** (v) to complete school or college successfully
> **obligation** (n) something that you have to do
> **occasions** (n) special events or ceremonies
> **personal** (adj) related to an individual person and not anyone else
> **thoughtful** (adj) showing care and consideration in how you treat other people

1 Did you really want to go to that dinner, or was it an _obligation_?
2 After I _graduate_ from college, I'm going to have a big celebration.
3 To make the card more _personal_, be sure to write a nice note inside.
4 To reward good _behavior_, Ms. Martinez lets her students have extra time outside.
5 Thank you for the flowers for our anniversary. That was really _thoughtful_
6 Becca likes to wear casual clothes. She only gets dressed up on special _occasions_.
7 Our company is having a special _event_ to honor its best salespeople.
8 Holidays have become too _commercial_. People spend too much on gifts.

USING YOUR KNOWLEDGE

2 Work in a small group. Discuss the questions.

92 the Parents and Friends by

1 On what occasions do people in your country usually give gifts? Who do they give gifts to? *birthdays – New baby and* *NEW* *Mother da*

2 Do you enjoy shopping for and giving gifts? Why or why not? *Yes Have Fun*

WHILE LISTENING

LISTENING FOR MAIN IDEAS

3 ▶ 4.6 Listen to the first part of the discussion. Circle the topic that the students are going to discuss.

a Is shopping fun?

b Are holidays too commercial?

c How do people celebrate Mother's Day?

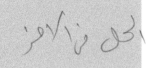

4 ▶ 4.7 Listen to the rest of the discussion. Do the speakers mention any of your ideas from Exercise 2, Question 1? Which ones?

_____

_____

TAKING NOTES ON DETAILS

5 ▶ 4.8 Listen to the discussion again and take notes about the speakers' *yes* and *no* arguments. Write the reasons people give for their opinion.

Have special occasions become too commercial?

yes	no
Davide	Yildiz

POST-LISTENING

SKILLS

Listening for opinion

When you listen, it is important to understand a speaker's opinion – that is, what the speaker thinks about a topic. To identify opinion, listen for phrases and expressions like these:

signposting an opinion	agreeing	disagreeing
It seems to me ...	I agree.	I'm not convinced.
What about ... ?	Yes, that's true.	I disagree.
Why not ... ?	That's right.	It's not true.
Personally, I ...	It's true.	I'm against ...
I think that ...	I couldn't agree more.	I don't agree.

6 ▶ 4.9 Listen and complete the opinion phrases.

1 I ___couldn't agree___ more.

2 How did this whole gift giving for every holiday tradition get started, anyway? It ___seems___ silly to me.

3 I ___agree___ . I get tired of shopping for gifts.

4 I ___disagree___ . I like giving gifts.

5 But I'm ___not convinced___ because then you have to spend money ... money that could be spent on more important things.

6 Instead, ___why not___ write letters of advice for the future? That would be more special.

7 Sorry, I ___don't agree___ . I doubt that graduates would be happy if we changed that custom!

DISCUSSION

7 Work in a small group. Think about Listening 1 and Listening 2 and answer the questions.

SYNTHESIZING

1 Do you think technology has changed gift-giving traditions? If so, how? Are these changes positive or negative?

2 What are your culture's customs for celebrating graduations? What is your opinion of these customs? Can you think of better ways to celebrate graduations?

3 Do you think most people buy gifts because it's an obligation or because they really want to? Which is true for you, or does it depend on the situation? Explain your answer.

SPEAKING

At the end of this unit, you will do the Speaking Task below.

▶ Take part in a discussion about whether special occasions have become too commercial.

▲ ANALYZE

1 Look at your notes from Listening 2. Match the arguments to the view they support. Write the arguments that you agree with from Listening 2 in the *I agree* row and the arguments you disagree with in the *I disagree* row.

	Special occasions have become too commercial.	Special occasions have not become too commercial.
I agree.	weddings	a lot of roses Food - قلبي عيد الاضحى يوم الطفل
I disagree.	because when you have be spend mony - mony that could be spent on More important things	

▲ REMEMBER

2 Work in a small group. Think of some more ideas for each side of the debate. Think about the holidays in your culture. Do you give gifts? Are those gifts meaningful? Are there any other events or occasions where people give gifts? Do you think giving these gifts is a good idea? Why or why not?

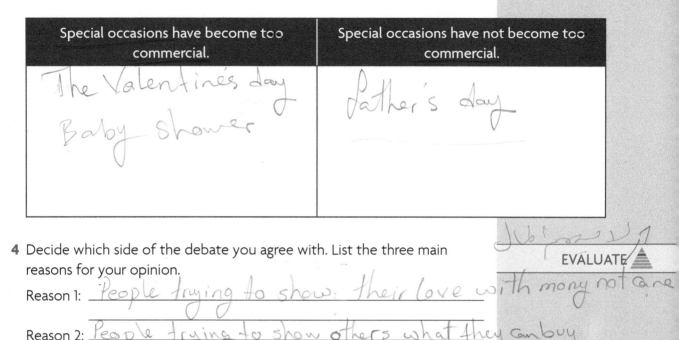

3 Write all of the ideas your group discussed in the chart.

Special occasions have become too commercial.	Special occasions have not become too commercial.
The Valentine's day Baby shower	Father's day

4 Decide which side of the debate you agree with. List the three main reasons for your opinion.

Reason 1: _People trying to show their love with money not care_

Reason 2: _People trying to show others what they can buy not how much they love each other_

Reason 3: _____

EVALUATE ▲

PREPARATION FOR SPEAKING

BEING POLITE IN A DISCUSSION

SKILLS

To have a good discussion, it is important to say when you agree and disagree with people. When you disagree, show that you understand and respect the other person's opinion.
You may be right, but ...
I see your point, but ...

You should also take turns and ask other peoples' opinions. You can do this by asking questions.
What do you think?
What's your opinion?

If you want to interrupt someone because you have a point to make, you can do it politely.
I'm sorry to interrupt, but ...
Excuse me for interrupting, but ...
Excuse me, can I say something?

1 Look at this discussion. Circle the best answers.

A: I think holidays are too commercial. What do you think?

B: (1) ~~I'm sorry to interrupt~~ / (I see your point,) but I think people really enjoy giving and receiving gifts. It's a way to show you care about people.

A: (2) ~~I agree~~ / (You may be right,) but there are better ways to show you care. It can be more thoughtful to spend time with people than to give them gifts.

B: (3) (I understand, but) / ~~You misunderstood my point~~ can't you do both? I mean, there's no reason that you have to choose –

A: (4) (I see your point) / ~~I'm sorry to interrupt,~~ but I actually do feel like it's a choice. Sometimes I'm so busy doing holiday shopping that I don't have enough time to spend with my friends and family.

B: I'm sorry, but (5) (I disagree) / ~~I understand.~~ I think if you plan ahead, and maybe shop online, shopping doesn't have to take a lot of time. You can give people nice gifts and also spend time with them.

2 Work with a partner. Follow the instructions.

Student A	Student B
• You think that it's good to relax on holidays. On special days, people should go out to dinner rather than cook. Cooking involves a lot of work, and no one should have to work on holidays. • Listen to Student B. • Tell Student B your opinion.	• Listen to Student A. • Say you understand, but traditions are تقاليد important. People have always made traditional food on special days, and they should continue to do that. Cooking is a way to show your family that you care about them. • Tell Student A your opinion.

USING ADVERBS FOR EMPHASIS

We can use adverbs to make a point stronger.

I <u>strongly</u> believe that people spend too much money on gifts. (= I believe very much)

I <u>really</u> think that ...

You can use these adverbs when you are sure that you agree or disagree.

I <u>totally</u> agree. (= I agree 100%.)

Yes, that's <u>completely</u> true.

That's <u>definitely</u> right.

I'm <u>really not</u> convinced. (= I have very big doubts about your point.)

It's <u>absolutely not</u> true.

3 Look at the sentences. Circle the sentences that you agree with and change the sentences you disagree with. Add adverbs if you have a strong opinion.

1 It's true that people don't have time to cook anymore.
   totally

2 I'm against spending a lot of money during holidays or celebrations.
   _____

3 I agree that modern technology has changed the way we interact with each other.
   totally

4 It's true that traveling to other countries helps us understand other cultures and their traditions.
   Completly believe that

5 I agree that tourists bring bad habits to our country.
   I absoluthy not

6 I don't believe that learning English affects local customs and traditions.
   I stronge mgt b elive that

4 Work with a partner. Compare your ideas from Exercise 3. Say if you agree or disagree with your partner.

PRONUNCIATION FOR SPEAKING

SKILLS

Stress patterns in phrases for agreeing and disagreeing

Speakers often stress adverbs for emphasis when they agree or disagree.

▶ 4.10 I **completely** agree that holidays have become too commercial.
I **absolutely** disagree that we should stop giving gifts on Mother's Day.
I **really** think that we should give fewer gifts.

5 Work with a partner. Underline the adverbs in the sentences. Then, practice saying the sentences. Remember to stress the adverbs.

1 I strongly believe that we should spend less time using social media.
2 I'm absolutely convinced that buying expensive cars is a waste of money.
3 I really think that we can learn a lot from older people.
4 I completely disagree with that argument.

PRISM Online Workbook

> Phrases with *that* can be used to introduce an opinion or an idea.
>
> I think <u>that</u> ... ,   I believe <u>that</u> ...
>
> Many people believe <u>that</u> ...   I doubt <u>that</u> ...

PRISM Online Workbook

6 Write *P* next to the sentences in which the speaker introduces a personal opinion. Write *O* next to the sentences in which the speaker refers to information from other people.

1 **I think that** it shows that you were thinking of someone. _P_

2 **I've heard that** when people receive more than a few gifts, they usually can't even remember who gave them which gift. _O_

3 **I believe that** we should learn about customs and traditions from different places. _P_

4 **Many people say that** travel improves the mind. _O_

5 **I disagree that** the Internet has destroyed local customs and traditions. _P_

6 **Everyone knows that** people usually buy gifts because it's an obligation, not because they really want to. _O_

7 **I doubt that** graduates would be happy if we changed that custom! _P_

8 **It's a well-known fact that** the Internet has made it easier to communicate. _O_

7 Complete the phrases with your own ideas.

1 I disagree that _you can show your love with money_.

2 I strongly believe that _being kind is more important than gift_s

3 It's a well-known fact that _women like shoes and bag_s

4 Everyone knows that _learning languages helps with traveling_

5 I've heard that _music could relax our body_ .

6 I doubt that _Money is important than health_ .

8 Work with a partner. Discuss your ideas from Exercise 7.

SPEAKING TASK

PRISM Online Workbook

> Take part in a discussion about whether special occasions have become too commercial.

PREPARE

1 Look at the chart you created in Exercises 3 and 4 in Critical Thinking. Review your notes and add any new information.

2 Work in a small group with students who have the same opinion as you. Look at the main points you want to make in the discussion and plan what language you will use to make these points. Make notes. You can use language like this:

It seems to me ...   أعتقد ذلك   I think that ...
What about ... ?   ماذا عن   I've heard that ...
Why not ... ?   لماذا لا   It's a well-known fact that ...
Personally, I ...

3 Make a list of arguments to support the opposite opinion. Then, make notes about how you will respond to each argument. You can use language like this:

I see your point, but ...   You may be right, but ...

4 Refer to the Task Checklist below as you prepare for your discussion.

TASK CHECKLIST	✔
Use adverbs for emphasis.	
Use phrases with *that* appropriately.	
Use suffixes and verbs and adjectives + prepositions appropriately.	
Interrupt, agree, and disagree appropriately.	
Show respect for other peoples' opinions.	

PRACTICE

5 Work in a group. Two people should agree with one side of the argument and two with the opposite side. Practice having your discussion. Take notes on the other students' performance during the practice and feedback to them on how they could improve their points.

DISCUSS

6 Discuss the topic with two other students from the opposite side and one from the same side.

ON CAMPUS

DEALING WITH CULTURE SHOCK

PREPARING TO LISTEN

1 You are going to listen to three students describing problems they had when they first arrived in North America to study. Before you listen, work in a small group and discuss the problems that students might have. What kinds of problems do you think international students might have with the following?

> classes   cultural behavior   food   language   weather

WHILE LISTENING

2 ▶ 4.11 Listen to the students' descriptions. Circle the topics in Exercise 1 that you hear.

3 ▶ 4.11 Listen to the descriptions again and circle the correct ending for each sentence.

1 Alisha was most upset because she couldn't _____
   a understand anything.
   b say what she wanted to.
   c take notes.

2 In her English classes, Alisha learned how to _____
   a make friends.
   b speak English better.
   c study in English.

3 John didn't like American food because _____
   a it made him sick.
   b it was too sweet.
   c it was too unhealthy.

4 Now John _____
   a likes American food.
   b likes cheese.
   c still eats Chinese food.

5 Minh thought that Americans _____
   a did not mean what they said.
   b were not polite.
   c were not friendly.

4 Work in a small group and discuss the questions.

1 How did each student manage to resolve their problem?
2 Have you ever had an experience like Alisha's, John's, or Minh's? If so, describe it.

Culture shock

Culture shock is a feeling of confusion that results from suddenly experiencing a culture that is not familiar. It is normal to feel culture shock, and the feelings of confusion will decrease with time.

PRACTICE

5 Work in a small group. Read the advice for dealing with culture shock. Match each sentence with a follow-up sentence.

1 Be patient. _____
2 Try not to judge the new culture or the people. _____
3 Keep yourself in shape. _____
4 Stay in touch with your friends and family at home. _____
5 Remember your personal goals. _____
6 Know where to go for help. _____

a But don't spend all of your free time texting and talking to them!
b Exercise is a good way to deal with stress.
c Give yourself time to adjust to your new environment.
d Most colleges have a tutoring center, an international student center, or counselors who can help you.
e Remind yourself often of the reasons why you came.
f The differences are cultural, not personal.

6 Work with a partner. Discuss the questions.

1 Which advice would have been useful for each of the students in Exercise 3?
2 Which three pieces of advice do you think are the most helpful?

REAL-WORLD APPLICATION

7 Work with a partner. Read the problems, and think of 2–3 pieces of advice for each person.

I don't understand anything the teachers say in class, and my English is not good enough to have conversations in English. There aren't many international students here – it's a small campus in a small town – and I feel very lonely. What can I do?

This is my first semester in the U.S. I like the college, but I don't like the classes. They're really easy! I learned this material in high school. The teachers are very informal, and in class we just have discussions. This isn't my idea of college. I don't feel like I'm learning anything.

8 Choose one of the situations from Exercise 7. Role-play a conversation between the student and a counselor.

LEARNING OBJECTIVES

Listening skills	Listen for attitude; identify references to common knowledge
Pronunciation	Attitude and emotion
Speaking skills	Use problem-solution organization; present persuasively using imperatives and adjectives
Speaking Task	Present an idea for a health product or program
On Campus	Stay in shape

ACTIVATE YOUR KNOWLEDGE

Work with a partner. Discuss the questions.

ماذا يفعلون ولماذا

1 What are the people in the photo doing? Why do you think they're doing it?

   ماذا لاعضاء لتخبذ الرياضة ..... منذ

2 What advice would you give to someone who wants to live to be 100 years old? What should the person do or not do?

3 Do you think it is easier or harder to stay healthy now than it was 100 years ago? Why?

   هل اعتقد الرجال الرياضة يصحوا صحة

PREPARING TO WATCH

ACTIVATING YOUR
KNOWLEDGE

1 Work with a partner. Discuss the questions. *I take a shower*

  1 What do you do to calm yourself when you feel angry or stressed?
  2 Have you ever tried to breathe slowly and deeply? How did it make you feel? *Yes, - I go to sleep*

PREDICTING CONTENT
USING VISUALS

2 Work with a partner. Look at the photos from the video and discuss the questions.

  1 What kind of class could this be?
  2 Where do you think the school is?
  3 Why do you think the students have their eyes closed?

GLOSSARY

courage (n) the ability to deal with dangerous or difficult situations without being frightened

yoga (n) a set of exercises for the mind and body, based on the Hindu religion

emotion (n) a strong feeling such as love or anger

focus (v) to pay attention to something

WHILE WATCHING

105

3 ▶ Watch the video. Circle the correct answers.

UNDERSTANDING MAIN IDEAS

1 The students think that yoga has _____ them.
   a helped   **b** bored   **c** excited

2 The program teaches yoga in _____ .
   a reading classes   **b** math classes   **c** school

3 Yoga connects your _____ , your feelings, and your body.
   a heart   **b** dreams   **c** mind

4 Most students say that after yoga they're more ready to _____ .
   a study   **b** learn   **c** work

5 Since the yoga classes began in the school, _____ have improved.
   a test scores   **b** physical fitness   **c** emotions

4 ▶ Watch the video again. Circle the words you hear.

UNDERSTANDING DETAILS

1 Sometimes it takes a lot of courage to just be a little bit more still and not *busy* / *happy*.

2 I forget about the *sad* / *bad* things that are happening.

3 I feel happy and *serious* / *calm*.

4 She first turned to yoga as *an overworked* / *a stressed-out* school teacher.

5 I think a real benefit is learning a process for internal *listening* / *studying*.

DISCUSSION

5 Work in a small group. Discuss the questions. Then, compare your answers with another group.

1 Are there programs in your school or workplace that teach relaxation? Describe them.

2 What activities can you think of that help:
   a our minds? Reading
   b our bodies? Jim- spor ...
   c our emotions? Music

3 What other activities can connect all three of these things?

مدرسة رياضة
النوم الجيد
جري

arden cultivation
زراعة الحديقة

106 as soon as

في أقرب وقت

PREPARING TO LISTEN

UNDERSTANDING
KEY VOCABULARY

1 You are going to listen to a radio program about why some people live a long life. Before you listen, read the sentences. Complete the definitions with the correct form of the words in bold.

1 My grandmother is very healthy. She's never had a serious **illness**.
2 Research **proves** that exercising can improve your health.
3 I have a **habit** of eating chocolate in the evenings. I eat it almost every night!
4 He doesn't have an **unhealthy** lifestyle. He always exercises and eats fruit and vegetables.
5 Exercise is important to me, so I **work out** at the gym three mornings a week.
6 I'm a few pounds **overweight**. I should probably go on a diet.

a ___4___ (adj) not good for your health; not strong and well
b ___5___ (phr v) to exercise in order to make your body stronger
c ___2___ (v) to show that something is true
d ___1___ (n) a disease of the body or mind
e ___6___ (adj) being heavier than you want or than is good for you
f ___3___ (n) something that you do regularly.

2 Work in a group and discuss the photos.

USING YOUR
KNOWLEDGE

1 What are the differences between the lifestyles of the people in the photos? B-C = healthy habits — A-D Not healthy
2 How do you think different lifestyles can affect our health?
3 Do you think that the genes we receive from our parents can affect our health? How? yes = my habits

unhealthy eating
and habits
bad?

WHILE LISTENING

3 ▶ 5.1 Listen to an introduction to a radio program and answer the questions.

1 Do people who live to be 100 years old always have a healthy lifestyle?

May not be enough.

2 What does the speaker say is more important than lifestyle for having a long and healthy life?

good genes. and sleep

+ postve
Negatv

4 ▶ 5.2 Listen to the radio program and complete the notes.

Speaker A

I think (1) *its great news Most People think that if They eat healthy food.*
I think that (2) *the key to a healthy life is to enjoy yourself.* (P+
I'd much rather (3) *go out and have a Pizza with friedes.* N—

Speaker B

It's ridiculous to (4) *get too worried about healthy eating and exercise* N—
I'm sure that (5) *genes are more important than our lifestyle~* P+

Speaker C

I prefer to (6) *exercise and eat well.* P+
I also think that (7) *you won't know whether or not you have the right genes.* P+
I'd say that (8) *its always better to have a healthy lifestyle.*
There's no doubt that (9) *bad healthy habits increase the chancese of getting* N— *a serious illnes.*

Speaker D

I'm sure that (10) *these children wont be able to enjoy a long and healthy.* N— 1½

I prefer to (11) *be cereful and take care of myself.* P+

C

D

SKILLS

Listening for attitude

To understand a speaker's message, it's necessary to understand their attitude — that is, what they are feeling or thinking. This is especially important in discussions, in which people might have different attitudes toward a topic.

To identify a speaker's attitude, listen for the speaker's use of:
- adjectives — are they positive or negative?
- sentence structure — using simple sentences or rhetorical questions?
- language — using figurative or common language?
- point of view — using the first or the third person?
- facts — stating general ideas or opinions rather than facts?

LISTENING FOR ATTITUDE

PRISM | Online Workbook

5 Work with a partner. Do you agree or disagree with the statement? Discuss your opinions and give reasons for them.

> Having a healthy lifestyle is *not* the most important thing if you want to live a long life.

6 Work with a partner. Look at your notes and discuss the questions.

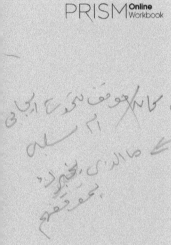

  1 Was the attitude of each speaker positive or negative.
  2 What tells you their attitude?

SKILLS

Attitude and emotion

You can often learn about a speaker's attitude from the sound of their voice. When a speaker is expressing strong feelings, their voice often goes up and down more than usual. Listen to the difference in the way the speaker says this sentence:

▶ 5.3

I'm really surprised about that. ↘ ⌒

I'm really surprised about that! ↗ —

In the first sentence, the speaker's goes down. He feels disappointed.
In the second sentence, the speaker's voice goes up. He feels excited.

7 ▶ 5.4 Listen to excerpts. How do you think each speaker feels about what they are saying? How do you know?

1 I think it's great news!
   The speaker feels _excited_ I know this because _____
   _____ intonation rises _____.

2 There's no question that happy people live longer.
   The speaker feels _Serben_ . I know this because _____
   _____.

3 It's ridiculous to get too worried about healthy eating and exercise!
   The speaker feels _Angry_ . I know this because _decless_
   _____.

4 Oh, that's great. So now we should all eat fast food and stop exercising?
   The speaker feels _Clam_ . I know this because _cynicel_
   _____.

5 Well, it's great that some people can live to be 100 and do whatever they want in their lives, but ...
   The speaker feels _obsf_ . I know this because _____
   _____.

Identifying references to common knowledge

Common knowledge means ideas that most people will probably agree with. Speakers often refer to common knowledge to make their arguments stronger. To express common knowledge, use phrases such as:

Everyone knows that ...   There is no doubt that ...

There is no question that ...   Most people think that ...

Sometimes speakers use these phrases with ideas that may not be completely true, or that may not be shared by everyone, to persuade the listener that they are right.

8 Work with a partner. Look at the sentences. Do you agree with each statement? Why or why not? Discuss your opinions.

1 **Most people think that** if they eat healthy food, they'll have a long, healthy life.
2 **There is no question that** happy people live longer.
3 **There is no doubt that** bad health habits increase the chances of getting a serious illness.
4 **Everyone knows that** exercise makes us happier.

DISCUSSION

9 Work with a partner. Discuss the questions.

1 Do you think your lifestyle is healthy? Why or why not? What could you do to make your lifestyle healthier?
2 Do you know any very old, healthy people? What kind of lifestyle do they have?
3 If you want to have a healthy lifestyle, what do you think are the most important things to do?

come on in = enter

PHRASAL VERBS

> LANGUAGE
>
> Phrasal verbs are two- or three-word verbs. They consist of a verb and one or two particles (small words like *up*, *out*, *in*). It is not always easy to understand the meaning of a phrasal verb by focusing only on the meaning of the verb and the particle(s). The parts together often have a completely different meaning than the individual parts.
>
> They spend hours **working out** at the gym.
> (*work out* = exercise to make your body stronger)

PRISM Online Workbook

1 Look at the sentences. Underline the phrasal verb in each sentence.

1 If you want to lose weight, you should <u>cut down on</u> fatty foods.
2 Last winter, I <u>came down with</u> four colds. I hope I'm healthier this year!
3 I want to try something new. Maybe I'll <u>take up</u> tennis.
4 Tim is going to <u>try out for</u> the soccer team. I don't think he'll make it, though; he's not a great player.
5 No matter how good their genes are, these children will not be able to enjoy a long and happy life unless they <u>give up</u> chips, chocolate bars, and sugary drinks.
6 Why don't you <u>sign up for</u> a yoga class? Yoga is good exercise, and it helps you relax.
7 Would you like to <u>join in</u> the game? You can be on our team.
8 It took me a long time to <u>get over</u> the flu. I was sick for two weeks.

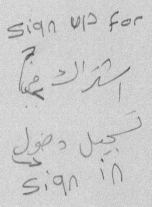

sign up for

اشتراك

تسجيل دخول

sign in

2 Write the phrasal verbs from Exercise 1 next to the correct definitions.

1 ___came down with___ to get an illness, especially one that is not serious
2 ___give up___ to stop a habit, often because it is unhealthy
3 ___sign up for___ to join a group or organization
4 ___join in___ to become involved in an activity with other people
5 ___try out for___ to compete for a position on a sports team or a part in a play
6 ___get over___ to become healthy again after having an illness
7 ___take up___ to start doing a particular job or activity
8 ___cut down on___ to eat or drink less of something

3 Complete the questions with phrasal verbs.

1 Have you ever ___give up___ a bad habit, like eating chocolate?

2 Have you ever had a cold or the flu? How long did it take you to ___get over___ it?

3 Have you ever ___sign up___ for exercise classes or for a gym membership?

4 Have you ___taken up___ any new activities in the past few years?

5 Have you ever ___tried out___ for a team?

6 Are there any foods that you want to ___cut down on___? Why do you want to eat less of these foods?

4 Work with a partner. Ask and answer the questions in Exercise 3. Ask follow-up questions to find out more information.

ADJECTIVES TO DESCRIBE WELL-BEING

5 Read the definitions. Complete the sentences with the correct form of the words in bold.

> **cultural** (adj) relating to the habits, traditions, and beliefs of a society
> **educational** (adj) relating to learning
> **emotional** (adj) relating to feelings
> **intellectual** (adj) relating to your ability to think and understand things, especially complicated ideas
> **personal** (adj) relating to a single person rather than to a group
> **physical** (adj) relating to the body
> **social** (adj) relating to activities in which you meet and spend time with other people

1 Exercising has ___emotional___ benefits. It can make you happier and calmer.

2 If you want to improve your ___social___ life, you should join a club to meet some new people.

3 Andrea is very ___intellectual___. She enjoys talking about literature and philosophy.

4 Max wanted to learn Spanish quickly, so he hired a ___personal___ tutor. He meets with his tutor twice a week for conversation practice.

5 ___Physical___ activity helps your body stay strong and healthy.

6 When you move to a new country, it can take some time to get used to the ___cultural___ differences.

7 Travel is fun, and it's also ___educational___. You can learn a lot about the history and culture of other places when you travel.

PREPARING TO LISTEN

UNDERSTANDING
KEY VOCABULARY

PRISM Online Workbook

1 You are going to listen to four presentations about programs that can improve your health. Before you listen, circle the best definition for each word in bold.

1 I don't feel like going to the gym this afternoon. I just want to stay home, **relax**, and watch movies.
   a to sleep
   b to review for a test
   c to become less stiff, tense, tight, or worried   صع اء

2 Marcus is feeling a lot of **stress** at work. It's giving him headaches.
   a worry caused by a difficult situation
   b a sickness caused by not getting enough sleep
   c energy you get from interacting with people   الصداع

3 Drinking a lot of water can be a good **treatment** for a stomachache.
   a a solution to a problem
   b something that you do to try to cure an illness or injury
   c something you can drink

4 If you **reduce** the number of calories you eat, you will lose weight.
   a to count the amount of something
   b to make (something) less in size, amount, etc.
   c to make (something) larger in size

5 Exercise has a number of **mental** benefits, like improving memory.
   a relating to the mind
   b relating to movement
   c relating to men

6 Eating healthy food can improve your athletic **performance**. It makes your muscles and bones stronger and helps you stay healthy.
   a how often a person does an activity
   b how well a person does an activity
   c how often a person wins

7 Writing requires a lot of **concentration**. It's a good idea to be alone in a quiet room when you're writing.
   a energy
   b the ability to be calm
   c the ability to give your whole attention to one thing

8 Anyone can **participate** on the team. You don't need to be an experienced player to join.
   a to take part in or become involved in an activity
   b to do something well
   c to stop doing something

USING YOUR
KNOWLEDGE

2 Work with a partner. Look at the photos. What do you think are the benefits of each activity? Discuss your ideas. *114*

meditation

1. Calm
2. Relief from day entens
3. Helping lose weight

team sports

1. fun for young people
2. healthy body sports

biking

sport for everyone

acupuncture

1. Pain relief
2. weight loss شاشی
3. disease treatment

صقل الإمراض

WHILE LISTENING

3 ▶ 5.5 Listen to the four presentations. What is each one describing?

a bike tour	acupuncture	a soccer club	meditation

Presentation 1: _meditation_
Presentation 2: _a soccer club_
Presentation 3: _a bike tour_
Presentation 4: _acupuncture_

4 ▶ 5.5 Listen again. What are the benefits of each program? Take notes.

Benefits of the health programs

Program 1 _the practice of thinking calm thoughts in order to relax._

Program 2 _physical fitness, and your team building skills_

Program 3 _educational fitness_

Program 4 _want to explore the secreture of traditional Chinese medicine._

DISCUSSION

5 Work in a small group. Use your notes from Listening 1 and Listening 2 to answer the questions.

1 What do you think each speaker in Listening 1 would think about the programs in Listening 2? Why?

2 Do you still agree with your answer to this question from the start of the unit?

> What advice would you give to someone who wants to live to be 100 years old? What should the person do or not do?

3 Do you want to try any of the activities in the presentations in Listening 2? Which ones? Why or why not?

SPEAKING

At the end of this unit, you will do the Speaking Task below.

> Give a presentation to a group of students about an idea for a health product or program.

SKILLS

Using idea maps

Idea maps are a good way to organize your notes as you listen. They help you see connections between the topic, the main ideas, and the details.

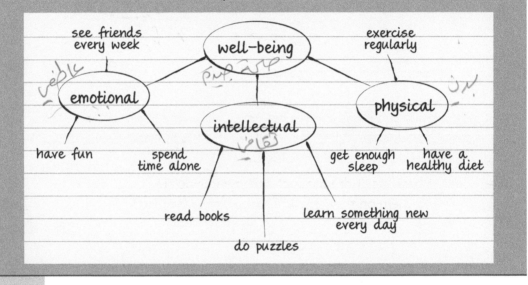

UNDERSTAND

1 Choose one of the programs from Listening 2 and complete the idea map.

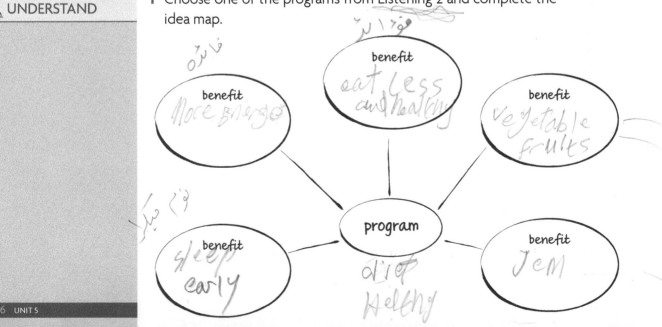

2 Work in a group. Brainstorm ideas for a health-related program that you might like to talk about. Write your ideas in the idea map.

sleeping well (well being)

Exeersige (physical) ③

Reading

(intellectual) قراءة

eating healthy (well being)

stay positive (emotional)

health-related programs

Stress

fewest

3 Look at the health programs you brainstormed in Exercise 2. Which has the most health benefits? Which has the fewest? Why? Choose one and write it in the center of the idea map below.

4 Think of some benefits of the product or program you are going to talk about and write them on the outside circles of the idea map.

EVALUATE

APPLY

Faces better

more

benefit
sleeping well

benefit
Helthy Body

benefit
stregnth قوة

benefit
Confidance ثقة

Excersice

benefit
less stress

happy life

Energetic طاقة

118

PROBLEM–SOLUTION ORGANIZATION

1 Work with a partner. Look at the script for a program presentation below and discuss the questions.

1 Why does the script begin with rhetorical questions?

To attract the listener attention

2 What effect do the rhetorical questions have on the listener?

_____

3 What three problems do the questions introduce?

_____

_____

4 What is the solution to the problems?

Meditation

5 What is the purpose of the part of the script that begins "As we all know"?

_____

6 Does the script explain what the treatment is good for?

yes

7 What information does the last part of the script provide?

Sanjee madikation

2 What is the organization of the presentation? Number the information.

- specific information about the place, time, etc. __4__
- background information about the program __3__
- rhetorical questions about the problems, to attract the listeners' attention __1__
- introduction of the solution __2__

Script for a program presentation

Do you feel tired? Are you under a lot of stress? Do you have problems concentrating on your work? If so, it's time to take up meditation — the practice of thinking calm thoughts in order to relax. As we all know, meditation can improve your health and your emotional well-being. It also has mental benefits — it has been shown to improve concentration. This ancient practice is known to increase your energy and lead to a happier life. Whether you are looking for a stress-free life, physical well-being, or self-discovery, Sanjee Meditation has it all. Sign up now for a free introductory class, starting on January 15th.

PRESENTING PERSUASIVELY

Speakers often try to persuade listeners to agree with them or to take action. Using rhetorical questions and identifying common knowledge are common persuasive techniques. Other persuasive techniques include:

1 **Using the imperative form.** The imperative form of a verb is strong and direct, so it is effective for persuasion. It is often used in advertisements.
Join us and **take advantage** of the many benefits of team sports.

2 **Using adjectives.** Adjectives help to persuade people by making them feel emotions.
So be **kind** to your body and your mind, and come with us on an **amazing** adventure you'll never forget!

3 Look at the excerpts from the product presentations. Underline the imperative verb forms.

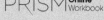

1 <u>Sign up</u> now for a free introductory class, starting on January 15th.
2 If you're interested in learning more about our group, <u>check out</u> our website at www.soccersundays.cup.com.
3 This spring, <u>join</u> our six-month course in acupuncture.
4 <u>Learn</u> more about the course and <u>visit</u> us on our open house days on the first Saturday of every month.

4 Work with a partner. Answer the questions.

1 What effect do the imperatives have on the listener?

_____

2 Why are imperatives used in the presentations?
to convince the buyer
_____

5 Make the sentences more persuasive by using imperative verb forms.

1 If you want, you can buy our new product.
Buy our new product!
2 It is possible to buy one and get one free.
buy one get one free
3 You should hurry and purchase a ticket now.
hurry and prchase a ticket now
4 People must not forget that our stores are open on holidays.
don't forget, our stores are open on holidays.
5 We would like you to register for our course before it's too late!
register for our _____

our side lesson

6 Look at the excerpts. Underline the adjectives. *120*

1 If so, it's time to take up meditation – the practice of thinking <u>calm</u> thoughts in order to <u>relax</u>.

2 Would you like to improve your social life, your <u>intellectual</u> <u>performance</u>, your physical fitness, and your <u>team-building</u> skills?

3 Not only does this trip provide <u>terrific</u> exercise and a <u>fascinating</u> cultural experience, it's the best way to learn.

4 Are you <u>interested</u> in alternative treatments?

5 Have you ever wanted to explore the secrets of <u>traditional</u> Chinese medicine?

6 It's also a great alternative for people who want to lose weight in an easy way. *dr*

7 Work with a partner. Discuss the questions.

1 Do the adjectives in Exercise 6 have a positive or negative meaning?

_____ *Positive* _____

2 What images come to your mind when you hear these adjectives?

_____ *good adjectives* _____

_____

3 Make a list of other adjectives you often hear in advertisements and persuasive presentations. Share these adjectives with the class.

_____ *Positive* _____

_____

SPEAKING TASK

PRISM Online Workbook

▶ Give a presentation to a group of students about an idea for a health product or program.

PREPARE

1 Look at the idea map you created in Exercise 4 in Critical Thinking. Review your notes and add any new information.

2 Make notes about what you will say. Use this organization:

1 rhetorical questions to introduce the problem and attract the listener's attention

2 introduction of the program and explanation of how it solves the problem

3 background information about the program

4 specific details about the place, time, and/or costs

3 Make a list of adjectives you will use to describe your program.

4 Make notes about common knowledge that you can use to help persuade your audience. You can use language like this:

Everyone knows that ...   There is no question that ...
There is no doubt that ...   Most people think that ...

5 Refer to the Task Checklist below as you prepare your presentation.

TASK CHECKLIST	✔
Use phrasal verbs correctly.	
Use adjectives to describe well-being correctly.	
Use problem–solution organization correctly.	
Use imperatives to persuade the listener.	
Use adjectives to persuade the listener.	

PRACTICE

6 Work in a small group. Take turns practicing your presentations. Take notes on your classmates' presentations.

PRESENT

7 Take turns giving your presentations to the class.

ON CAMPUS

STAYING IN SHAPE

PREPARING TO LISTEN

1 You are going to listen to an interview with a health expert about staying in shape. Before you listen, look at the questions and check the boxes.

Do you ...	no / not usually	sometimes	yes, usually
1 get regular aerobic exercise (e.g., walking, swimming)?			
2 play a sport?			
3 eat healthy food?			
4 drink water regularly?			
5 get at least seven hours of sleep every night?			

2 Work in a small group. Compare your answers. Then, discuss the questions.

1 Are you generally in good health?
2 Why is it important for students to be in good physical health?
3 Why is it sometimes difficult for students to have a healthy lifestyle?

WHILE LISTENING

3 ▶ 5.6 Listen to the interview. Circle the main point about college students.

a They are under a lot of stress.
b They need to learn time management skills.
c They should get more exercise.
d They need to get more sleep.

4 ▶ 5.6 Listen to the interview again. Write *T* (true) or *F* (false) according to the interview. Correct the false sentences.

_____ 1 Mirna Pham wrote a book about health.
_____ 2 Many students feel stress because their classes are difficult.
_____ 3 Most students have good health habits.
_____ 4 Exercise helps the brain work better.
_____ 5 Most people need at least 9 hours of sleep every night.
_____ 6 People who exercise usually have other good habits.
_____ 7 Healthy habits begin in college.

PRACTICE

5 Work with a partner. Look at the ideas in the boxes. What cause and effect relationships can you find? Describe them.

If you have a busy schedule, you might stay up late and eat badly. If you get exercise, you can sleep well. As a result, ...

THE STRESS CYCLE
busy schedule   stay up late   eat badly   feel tired in class
feel stressed   have no free time

THE EXERCISE CYCLE
get exercise   study better   sleep well   eat healthy food
feel less stress   feel happier

6 Have you experienced either of these patterns? Describe your experiences.

REAL-WORLD APPLICATION

7 Look at the ways to keep fit and healthy in college. Work in a small group and discuss the questions.

> play on a university sports team
> run a marathon or half-marathon
> take fitness classes for credit
> take group camping and hiking trips
> walk or bike to class
> wear a device to monitor your fitness levels, nutrition, and sleep
> work out at a gym

1 Which of the activities do you do now?
2 Which do you think are most effective?
3 What other ways of keeping fit are possible where you live?

8 Choose one of the activities above. Research what is available at your school or in your city. Consider:

Convenience: Where and when can students do this activity?
Cost: How much does it cost? Is special equipment needed?
Other obstacles: How could you overcome them?

9 Present the results of your research to the class.

Listening skills	Understand references to earlier ideas; understand lecture organization
Pronunciation	Weak and strong forms
Speaking skills	Preview a topic; organize ideas; explain how something is used
Speaking Task	Give a presentation about an invention or discovery that has changed our lives
On Campus	Use visuals

DISCOVERY AND INVENTION

ACTIVATE YOUR KNOWLEDGE

Racing car

Work with a partner. Discuss the questions.

1 The photo shows a very early computer. When do you think it was invented?

2 There is a saying that "necessity is the mother of invention." What do you think this means?

3 What famous inventions or discoveries come from your country?

4 What do you think is the most important invention or discovery in the last 20 years? Why is it important?

PREPARING TO WATCH

ACTIVATING YOUR KNOWLEDGE

1 Work with a partner. Discuss the questions.

1 What can we make with 3D printers? Are these things expensive?
2 Why do some people need artificial body parts, or prosthetic replacements?
3 Can you think of any famous people with prosthetic replacements?

PREDICTING CONTENT USING VISUALS

2 Work with a partner. Look at the photos from the video and discuss the questions.

1 What can the boy do with the prosthetic hand?
2 How do you think the boy feels about the hand?
3 What role does the college student in the fourth photo play in this situation?

GLOSSARY

device (n) a piece of equipment that is used for a particular purpose

prosthetic replacement (n phr) an artificial body part, for example one that takes the place of an arm or foot

wrist (n) the part of your body between your hand and your arm

grip (n) a tight, strong hold on something, usually with your hand

take for granted (idm) to expect something and not understand that you are lucky to have it

pay off (phr v) to bring success, especially after hard work and a period of time

crowdfunding (n) collecting money for a particular purpose from a large group of people, often by asking for help on the Internet

---

WHILE WATCHING

3 ▶ Watch the video. Complete the paragraph with the words in the box.

3D college expensive new normal prosthetic successful

Holden Mora is showing the reporter his (1) _Prostheti_ hand. Normally, a hand like this would be very (2) _expensive_ but a (3) _college_ student made this one for $20 using a (4) _3D_ printer. He wanted Holden to be able to do (5) _normal_ things like hold a bottle or a knife and fork. The project was so (6) _successf_ that 11 other children are now waiting for their (7) _new_ hands.

4 ▶ Watch the video again. Correct the sentences.

1 Holden Mora is 17 years old.
   _7_

2 Jeff Powell built the hand using instructions from his professor.
   on the

3 The printer builds the parts in 44 hours.
   _24_

4 Holden cannot pick up things with his artificial hand.
   can

5 Holden is now raising money to build hands for other kids.
   Jeff Powell

6 Holden hopes other teachers can have the best kind of hands, too.
   children

DISCUSSION

5 Work in a small group. Discuss the questions. Then, compare your answers with another group.

1 Think of something in your life that was physically very difficult for you to do. How did you learn to do it?

2 Are you surprised by how happy and excited the boy in the video is? Why or why not?

3 Have you ever used a 3D printer? What would you build with one?

LISTENING

PREPARING TO LISTEN

UNDERSTANDING
KEY VOCABULARY

1 You are going to listen to a museum tour about inventions in the Middle Ages. Before you listen, read the definitions. Complete the sentences with the correct form of the words in bold.

> **design** (v) to make or draw plans for something
> **develop** (v) to make something over a period of time
> **device** (n) a piece of equipment that is used for a specific purpose
> **diagram** (n) a simple picture that shows how something works or what it looks like
> **discover** (v) to find information, a place, or an object, especially for the first time
> **invent** (v) to create something that had never been made before
> **scientific** (adj) relating to the study of science
> **technology** (n) knowledge, equipment, and method used in science and industry

1 Al-Jazari _develop_ machines to help with farming. He made drawings and gave detailed descriptions of how to build these machines.
2 _Scientific_ research has proven that genes can affect our health.
3 Scientists hope to someday _discover_ a cure for cancer.
4 The Chinese _invented_ gunpowder and used it for weapons.
5 A baby monitor is a _device_ that lets parents watch their baby when they're in a different room.
6 The Wright brothers _design_ the airplane in 1903.
7 This _diagram_ isn't very clear. I can't figure out how to put this together!
8 Modern _technology_ such as computers and cell phones have changed our lives.

2 Match the photos with the inventions. What do you think each invention is used for?

129

1 the fountain pen ___D___
2 eyeglasses ___C___
3 gunpowder ___a___
4 the crankshaft ___b___

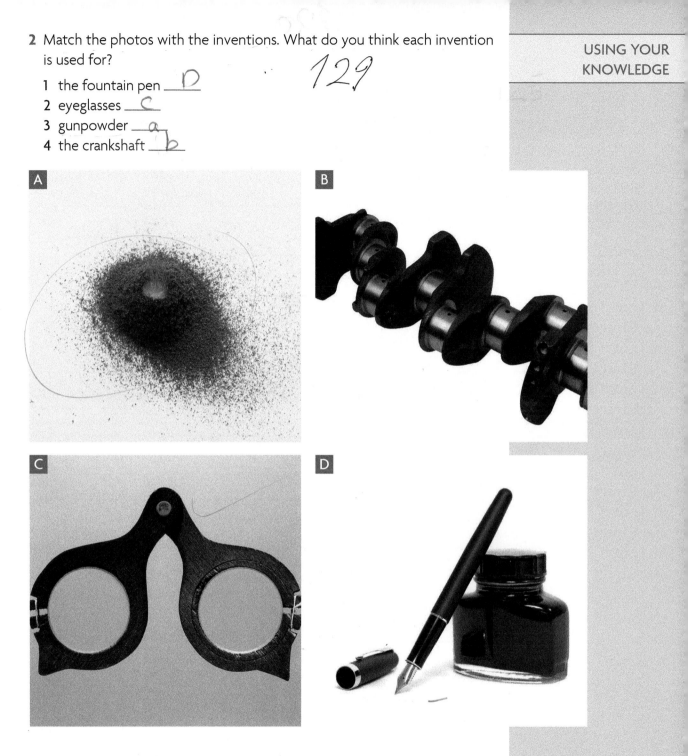

WHILE LISTENING

3 ▶ 6.1 Listen to a museum tour that mentions the inventions from Exercise 2. Number the inventions in the order they are mentioned.

the fountain pen ___1___
eyeglasses ___2___
gunpowder ___4___
the crankshaft ___3___

TAKING NOTES ON DETAILS

4 ▶ **6.1** Listen to the tour again and complete the notes about the inventions.

invention	when it was invented	where it was invented	who invented it	why it was invented
fountain (1) _pen_	(2) _953_	(3) _Africa_	unknown	so people wouldn't get (4) _cure_ on their fingers
(5) _eye glasses_	(6) _13_ century	(7) _italy_	unknown	to help people (8) _with bad vision_
crankshaft	(9) _12_ century	(10) _Turkey_	Al-Jazari, a great (11) _engineer_	to water (12) _____ and fields on (13) _farms_ (now used in (14) _car_ engines)
gunpowder	(15) _9_ century	(16) _china_	(17) _scientists_	to try to (18) _live_ forever

POST-LISTENING

SKILLS

Understanding references to earlier ideas

To refer to things they talked about earlier, speakers often use words such as *it, he, she, they, then,* and *there*. This sounds better than repeating the same information.

In this sentence, the word **it** refers to the invention of the telephone:

In 1876, Bell invented the telephone. ← It changed the way we communicate.

5 Look at the sentences. Underline the words that the words in bold refer to.

1 The first fountain pen was made in 953 in Africa. Before **then**, people used bird feathers and ink to write with.

2 As some of you may know, the Middle Ages have often been called the "Dark Ages". During this tour, you will find out that **they** were not.

3 Eyeglasses were invented In Italy in the thirteenth century. No one knows who invented **them**.

4 The invention of gunpowder has changed the way we fight wars. **It** changed the outcome of many medieval battles and affected the history of the world.

SKILLS

Weak and strong forms

In spoken English, small words (such as *a, an, the, do, does, to, from, at, of*) are not usually stressed. When these words are unstressed, they're called *weak forms*.

The unstressed vowel in these weak forms is pronounced /ə/ (*to* = /tə/, *the* = /ðə/, etc.).

However, speakers sometimes stress these small words to make them the main part of their message. When these words are stressed, they're called *strong forms*.

PRISM Online Workbook

6 ▶ 6.2 Listen and complete the sentences with weak forms.

1 Inventions __and__ technology from India, China, North Africa, __and__ __the__ Middle East were brought __to__ Europe,

2 __the__ first eyeglasses were held in front __of__ __the__ eyes or balanced on __the__ nose.

3 __the__ crankshaft is __a__ long arm that allows machines __to__ move __in__ __a__ straight line.

4 As we move along, you'll find one __of__ __the__ most important inventions __of__ medieval times.

7 ▶ 6.3 Listen to the excerpts. Match them to the reasons for using strong forms.

1 The Middle Ages **were** an interesting time, and they were full of scientific discoveries. __b__

2 Inventions and machines designed by medieval scholars made a great contribution to society, and many are still in use today. **And** some of these inventions are very common. __c__

3 Many people think gunpowder is **the** most important invention in history. __a__

Strong forms are used ...

a to emphasize that there is nothing better or more than this.

b to contrast with an earlier idea that the Middle Ages were **not** an interesting time.

c to emphasize that there is more information.

DISCUSSION

8 Look at the photos of some Chinese inventions. Think about the questions and make notes.

1 How have these inventions changed the history of the world?
2 Are they still used? How?
3 Have these inventions led to other discoveries? Which ones?
4 Which invention do you think is the most important? Why?

9 Work in a group. Take turns explaining why the invention you chose is the most important.

the compass

making paper

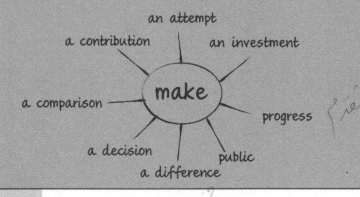

printing

◉ LANGUAGE DEVELOPMENT

USES OF THE VERB *MAKE*

The verb *make* has three main meanings: "force," "cause," or "produce."

Force: My boss **made** me work late last night.

Cause: Water and weights **make** the mechanical clocks work.

Produce: The first fountain pen was **made** in 953.

Make is also used in phrases with many nouns. These include:

an attempt
a contribution
an investment
a comparison — **make** — progress
a decision
public
a difference

133

1 Look at the sentences. What is the meaning of *make* in each sentence? Write *cause*, *force*, or *produce*.

1 Gunpowder was first **made** in China. ___produce___

2 My professor **made** me rewrite my assignment because there were too many mistakes. ___force___

3 Social media **makes** it easy for people to stay in touch. ___cause___

4 Today, most pens are **made** of plastic. ___produced___ 8.4

5 The new discovery **made** a lot of people very happy. ___cause___

6 I **made** myself stay up late to finish the work. ___force___

2 Circle the best definition for each phrase in bold.

1 If you **make a comparison** between these two TVs, you'll see that this one has a much clearer picture.
   a to consider the benefits of something
   b to consider the similarities between two things

2 I like both of these phones a lot. It's hard to **make a decision** about which one to buy.
   a to choose
   b to know

3 Inventions and machines designed by medieval scholars **made a great contribution** to society.
   a to give money
   b to help to make something successful

4 The invention of the lightbulb **made a** huge **difference** in people's lifestyles. After it was invented, life was never the same.
   a to remove something
   b to change something

5 For over a century, inventors have been **making attempts** to create a car that can fly, but they haven't succeeded.
   a to try
   b to fail

6 About ten years ago, Andrew **made a** smart **investment** in a tech start-up company, and now he's a millionaire.
   a to start a small business
   b to put money into something to make a profit

7 This is a good smartphone, but they could still **make improvements** to it. For example, I wish it had a better battery life.
   a to make something better
   b to make something more expensive

8 The company announced that it's going to be acquired, but the identity of the buyer hasn't been **made public** yet. They'll share that information later this month.
   a to share information about
   b to make a presentation

LANGUAGE DEVELOPMENT 133

PASSIVE VERB FORMS

> **Passive sentences** focus on what happened to something or someone.
> **Active sentences** focus on who or what did something.
> Passive: **The digital computer** was invented in 1936. (focuses on the invention)
> Active: **Alan Turing** invented the digital computer. (focuses on the inventor)
>
> To form the simple past of the passive, use *was/were* + past participle.
> Use *by* when it's important to know who did something.
> The lightbulb was developed **by** Edison.

PRISM Online Workbook

3 Work with a partner. Look at the list of inventors and inventions. Write each sentence in the passive form.

1 Apple's first tablet computer – develop – the 1990s
   Apple's first tablet computer was developed in the 1990s.

2 the law of gravity – discover – Isaac Newton – the seventeenth century
   was ed in

3 the first computer chip – invent – the 1950s
   was ed in

4 the first smartphone – create – after 1997
   Was d

5 penicillin – first produce – 1928 – Alexander Fleming
   was d in by

4 Complete the sentences using the correct form of the verbs in parentheses. Use active or passive forms.

1 Paper Was discovered (discover) in ancient China.
2 The telephone was invented (invent) in 1876.
3 Imhotep, an Egyptian architect, was designed (design) the pyramid of Djoser.
4 Eyeglasses were developed (develop) to help people with bad vision to read.
5 This letter was written (write) with ink.
6 A very early calculator was created (create) by Blaise Pascal.
7 Millions of people download (download) smartphone apps every day.
8 The pictures was sent (send) by text.
9 The first photograph was taken (take) in 1826.
10 Edison developed (develop) his first lightbulb in 1879.

LISTENING 2

PREPARING TO LISTEN

1 You are going to listen to a lecture about the history of smartphone apps. Before you listen, read the definitions. Complete the sentences with the correct form of the words in bold.

> **access** (v) to be able to enter or use something
> **allow** (v) to make it possible for someone to do something
> **app** (n) (abbreviation for *application*) software designed for a particular purpose that you can download onto a smartphone or other mobile device
> **create** (v) to make something new, or invent something
> **industry** (n) the companies and activities involved in the process of producing goods for sale
> **install** (v) to put new software onto a computer or mobile device
> **product** (n) something that is made to be sold
> **users** (n) people who use a product, machine, or service

2 b—

3 u.s.

1 I need a password to _access_ the Wi-Fi connection in this café.
2 Once you download the _app_ , you have to _install_ it on your smartphone.
3 This software lets you _create_ your own apps. I have some great ideas I'd like to try!
4 In a recent study, 45% of American smartphone _users_ said they would rather give up their vacations than their phone.
5 I always read _product_ reviews before I buy an expensive item.
6 IT (information technology) is an extremely fast-growing _industry_
7 Smartphones _allow_ us to stay in touch with each other constantly.

2 Work in a small group and discuss the questions.

1 Approximately how many apps do you have on your phone? How often do you install new ones? Which apps do you use most often? _not often_ _Dictionary_

40 ←

2 How many apps do you think are downloaded every year worldwide? _more than_ _1m_

3 What are some ways in which smartphones and apps have changed people's lives?

LISTENING FOR MAIN IDEAS

شكر شكل شخص

ه قصائد وكالة ك
ملايين ا

3 ▶ 6.4 Listen to an introduction to a lecture. Number the topics in the order that they will be discussed.

a The influence of apps on our lives _2_
b Specific examples of popular apps _3_
c The history of apps _1_

4 Make a list of the five types of smartphone apps that you think are the most useful.

1 Dictionary
2 youtube
3 face Book ✓

4 coogle
5 whatsApp

5 ▶ 6.5 Listen to the lecture. Check the types of apps you listed in Exercise 4 that the speaker mentioned.

TAKING NOTES ON DETAILS

6 ▶ 6.5 Listen to the lecture again and complete the notes.

first apps used for:
- accessing the (1) the internet
- (2) check emails ✓
- (3) send texts ✓

second gen. apps:
- (4) the frest app Store was opened in 2008
- 2011 – 10 billion downloads
    - people used more apps than (5) internet browsers
- by 2015 – (6) 100 billion app been downloads

road trip before smartphones: (7)
week before the trip .
go to library to get some guide Books .
    goto the store buy some maps كتب

road trip after smartphones: (8)
one smart phone does it all
The GPS would rplace the directions and map

another effect of apps:
- there is a need for skilled (9) software engineers ,

negative effects of apps:
- people are more (10) helples
- people are less (11) Patient

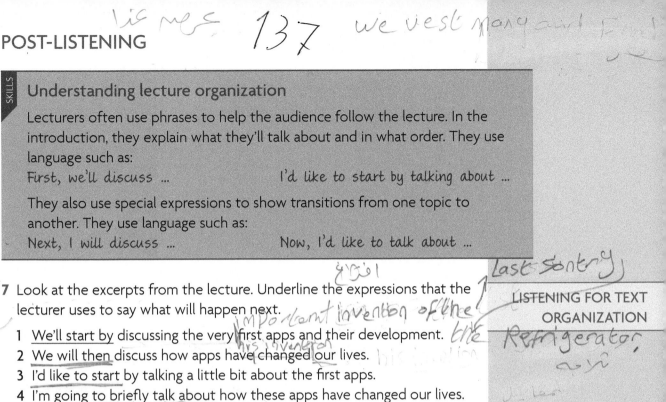

SKILLS

Understanding lecture organization

Lecturers often use phrases to help the audience follow the lecture. In the introduction, they explain what they'll talk about and in what order. They use language such as:

First, we'll discuss ...   I'd like to start by talking about ...

They also use special expressions to show transitions from one topic to another. They use language such as:

Next, I will discuss ...   Now, I'd like to talk about ...

7 Look at the excerpts from the lecture. Underline the expressions that the lecturer uses to say what will happen next.

1 <u>We'll start by</u> discussing the very first apps and their development.

2 We will then discuss how apps have changed our lives.

3 I'd like to start by talking a little bit about the first apps.

4 I'm going to briefly talk about how these apps have changed our lives.

5 Now I'd like to mention another important effect of the invention of apps.

6 In the next part of the lecture, I will discuss some of the most common apps in more detail.

DISCUSSION

8 Work in a small group. Think about Listening 1 and Listening 2 and answer the questions.

1 The speaker in Listening 1 stated that, "Many people think gunpowder is *the* most important invention in history." Do you agree? Is it more important than the invention of the smartphone? Why or why not?

2 If you could invent anything (including an app), what would you invent? Why?

3 Technology has developed rapidly in the last century. Do you think its development is slowing now? Why or why not?

4 What do you think will be the most important invention in the next 25 years?

LISTENING FOR TEXT ORGANIZATION

SYNTHESIZING

CRITICAL THINKING

138

[handwritten Arabic notes]

At the end of this unit, you will do the Speaking Task below.

Give a short presentation about an invention or discovery that has changed our lives.

SKILLS

Researching a topic using *Wh-* questions and idea maps

When you do research on a topic, ask yourself the following questions:
Who? What? When? Where? Why? Many researchers add *How?* to this list.
Then search for the answers to these questions. To organize your research, it is helpful to make an idea map like the one in Exercise 1.

▲ UNDERSTAND

1 Choose one of the inventions from Listening 1 or one of the apps from Listening 2. Complete the idea map for the invention. Use information from your notes on page 130 or 136.

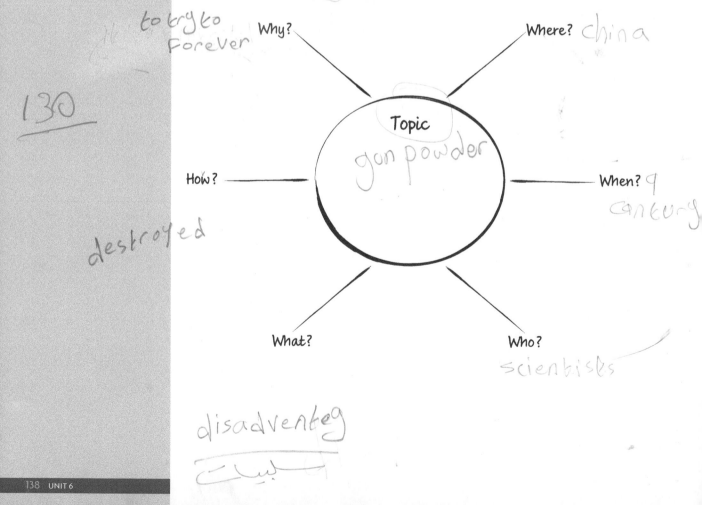

to try to Forever

130

Why?

Where? china

Topic
gun powder

How?

When? 9
century

destroyed

What?

Who?
scientists

disadventeg

[handwritten Arabic]

2 Choose an invention to talk about in the Speaking Task. You can talk about one of the inventions in the photos below or use your own idea.

the credit card

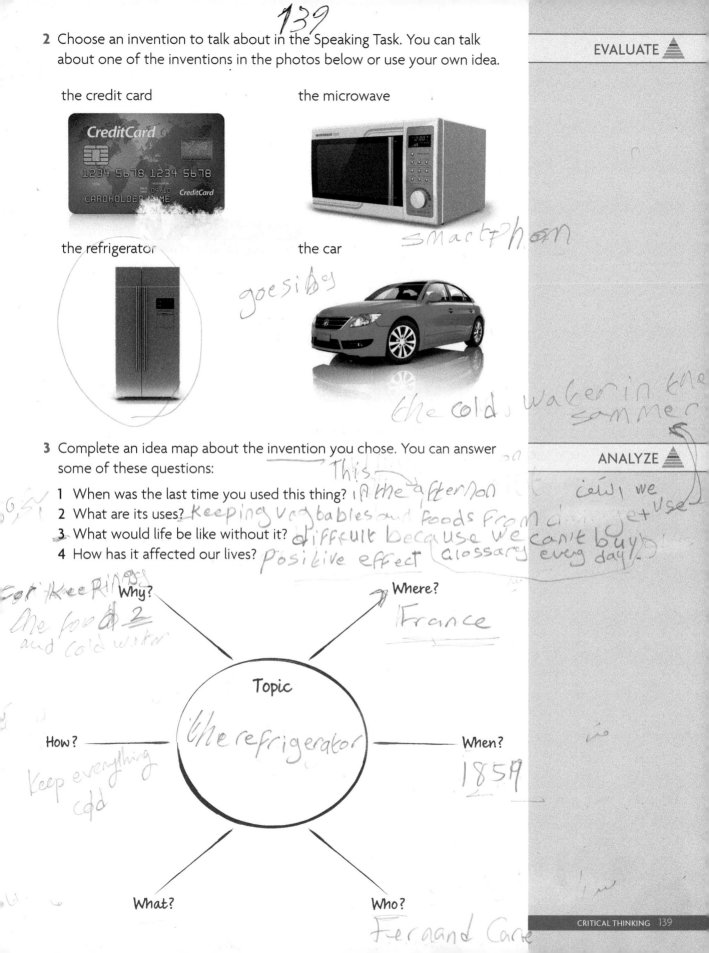

[handwritten: smactphon]

the microwave

the refrigerator

the car

[handwritten: goesiby]

[handwritten: the cold water in the summer]

3 Complete an idea map about the invention you chose. You can answer some of these questions:

1 When was the last time you used this thing? *[handwritten: This in the afternon]*
2 What are its uses? *[handwritten: Keeping vagbables and foods from ... get use]*
3 What would life be like without it? *[handwritten: Difficult because we can't buy Glossary every day]*
4 How has it affected our lives? *[handwritten: Positive effect]*

[handwritten: we]

[handwritten: for keeping the food 2 and cold water]

Why?

Where?
[handwritten: France]

Topic
[handwritten: the refrigerator]

How? *[handwritten: Keep everything cold]*

When?
[handwritten: 1859]

What?

Who?
[handwritten: Feraand Care]

PREVIEWING A TOPIC   *140*

SKILLS

In the introduction to a presentation, give a preview of what you will talk about. This helps your audience follow your talk. Here are some examples of language you can use to preview a topic:

I'd like to start by talking about ...   After that, I'm going to explain ...
Then, I'll discuss ...   Finally, I'll explore ...

sorry for being late

1 ▶ 6.6 Listen to an introduction to a presentation that previews what the speaker will talk about. Check the things that the speaker does.

 1 mentions the invention's name in the first sentence ☑
 2 gives a description of the invention ☑
 3 says how you can use it ☑
 4 gives specific details on how this invention is used ☑
 5 explains what will happen next in the presentation ☒

2 Work with a partner. Practice giving an introduction about a simple invention. Use the preview below to organize your ideas.

Student A: give an introduction to a presentation about the **paper notebook**.

Student B: give an introduction to a presentation about the **ballpoint pen**.

I would like to present an invention that has changed the way we _used to write_ . It's a simple invention, and we have all used it.
It's the _paper notebook_
A _paper notebook_ is _too many papers stick together_
(*explain the invention here*)
You can _write on a page and turn to the other page_.
(*explain how it is used in general*)
First, I am going to talk about _____ . Then, I will explain how it has improved our lives.

how we used to write on seperat pages and we usually lost some of them

ORGANIZING IDEAS

Before you write a presentation outline, decide in what order you will present your ideas. This will help you make sure that your ideas are in a logical order before you start writing. For example, it is logical to tell your listeners background information before you tell them why something is useful. You can use *Wh-* questions to organize your presentation.

3 Read the next part of the presentation. Number questions in the order they are answered in the presentation.

PRISM Online Workbook

a Why do people use them? __6__
b Who invented them? __2__
c Where can people use them? __5__
d Why were they invented? __3__
e When were they invented? __1__
f What is the best thing about the invention? __7__
g When were they first sold? __4__

To start with, Post-it® notes were invented in 1974 by Art Fry. Fry needed a bookmark that would stay inside the book and didn't fall out. He used a special type of glue invented by his colleague Spencer Silver. The glue was not very strong and made it easy to remove the notes.

In 1977, the first Post-it® notes were sold in stores. Since then, they have become a global phenomenon. People all over the word recognize the small, yellow sticky notes. We use them at work, at school, and at home.

Because the glue does not leave any stains, people can stick Post-it® notes anywhere. They allow us to remember important information and take notes. The best thing is that you can stick a Post-it® note anywhere to help you remember something.

EXPLAINING HOW SOMETHING IS USED

We can use the words and expressions in bold to talk about how something is used.
Post-it® notes **help people to** remember things.
Without the crankshaft, car engines wouldn't work.
The microwave **makes it** possible to cook food quickly.
Social media **is useful for** communicating with friends.
The lightbulb **allows us to** see at night.

PRISM Online Workbook

4 Complete the sentences with phrases from the box.

| allows us | are useful for | helps people to | makes it | without |

1 GPS _allows us_ to find our way around unknown places.
2 The cell phone _are useful for_ stay in touch.
3 Translation apps _helps people to_ learning another language.
4 Television _makes it s_ easy to learn about the world.
5 _without_ the computer chip, we wouldn't be able to use laptops.

5 Write two sentences about the laptop computer and two sentences about the smartphone. Use phrases from Exercise 4.

laptop
it is Used anywhere for ease carrying
Stores information for immediate Use

smartphone
Make commuication easy between People any wher
Easy to ask for help and quick rescue

6 Work with a partner. Take turns saying your sentences.

Home work

SPEAKING TASK

Give a short presentation about an invention or discovery that has changed our lives.

PREPARE

1 Look at the idea map you created in Exercise 3 in Critical Thinking. Review your notes and add any new information. Decide in what order you'll answer the *Wh-* questions. Write the questions in order below.

1 _____
2 _____
3 _____
4 _____
5 _____

2 Make some notes about the language you will use. You can use language like this:

To preview your topic
I'd like to start by talking about ...
Then, I'll discuss ...
After that, I'm going to explain ...
Finally, I'll explore ...

To explain how something is used
_____ helps people to ...
Without _____ , ...
_____ makes it _____ to ...
_____ is useful for ...

3 Refer to the Task Checklist below as you prepare your presentation.

TASK CHECKLIST	✔
Use phrases with *make* correctly.	
Preview the topic clearly.	
Organize your ideas in a logical order.	
Explain clearly how something is used.	

PRACTICE

4 Work with a partner. Take turns practicing your presentation. Take notes during your partner's presentation.

PRESENT

5 Work in a small group. Take turns giving your presentations. Discuss which one of your inventions has had the biggest influence on our lives.

USING VISUALS

PREPARING TO LISTEN

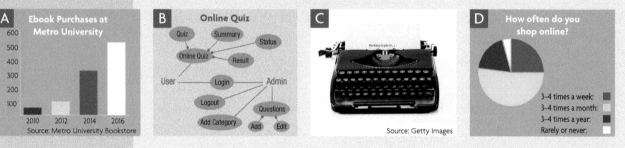

A Ebook Purchases at Metro University
Source: Metro University Bookstore

B Online Quiz

C Source: Getty Images

D How often do you shop online?
3–4 times a week:
3–4 times a month:
3–4 times a year:
Rarely or never:

1 You are going to listen to four excerpts from some student presentations. Before you listen, look at the visual aids. What does each one show?

2 Which visual aid is used ...

1 to compare data? _____
2 to show percentages? _____
3 to show how something works? _____
4 to show what something looks like? _____

3 Work with a partner. Discuss the questions.

1 How do visual aids help a presentation?
2 What other kinds of visual aids can you think of?

WHILE LISTENING

4 ▶ 6.7 Listen to the excerpts. Match each presentation to the visual aid that is being used.

1 _____   2 _____   3 _____   4 _____

5 ▶ 6.7 Listen to the excerpts again and match the expressions you hear to the excerpts. You will hear some expressions more than once.

	Excerpt 1	Excerpt 2	Excerpt 3	Excerpt 4
This is ...				
This chart/diagram shows ...				
This chart gives information about ...				
As you can see ...				
We can see that ...				

Using visual aids in a presentation

- Make sure that the visual is clear and easy to see from all parts of the room.
- Simplify data to show only the most important points.
- Name the source of the information.
- Use expressions like *As you can see, ...* to refer to visuals.

PRACTICE

6 Work with a partner. Look at the list below. Write what type of visual you would use to illustrate each item.

7 Look at the list below again. Write what you would say to refer to the visual in each case.

1 How a bicycle is made: _diagram_

   The diagram shows how a bicycle is made.

2 How adults and teenagers use the Internet: _____

   _____

3 How a solar panel works: _____

   _____

4 The first personal computer: _____

   _____

5 The percentage of students who use different types of transportation:

   _____

   _____

6 A new type of running shoe: _____

   _____

7 The market share of six popular apps: _____

   _____

8 Use of the Internet in ten different countries: _____

   _____

REAL-WORLD APPLICATION

8 Prepare to present a visual to your group. Do the following:

1 Choose two topics from exercise 6.
2 Find one good visual aid to illustrate each topic. Use a different kind of visual for each topic: photograph, diagram, chart, etc.
3 Reproduce each visual on a slide, using slide show presentation software. If necessary, simplify the information to show the most important points.
4 Write the name of the source at the bottom of the slide.

9 Work in a small group and present your visuals. Which visuals are most effective? Why?

LEARNING OBJECTIVES

Listening skills	Take notes on main ideas and details; auxiliary verbs for emphasis
Pronunciation	Vowel omission
Speaking skills	Ask for opinions and check information; ask follow-up questions
Speaking Task	Take part in an interview
On Campus	Plan assignments

ACTIVATE YOUR KNOWLEDGE

Work with a partner. Discuss the questions.   *cat walk*

1 What are the people in the photo doing?

2 Is fashion important to you? Why or why not?

3 What do young people like to wear in your country at the moment?

4 Has fashion changed a lot in your country in the last 50 years? How has it changed?   *clomit change*

5 What do you think are some reasons why fashions change?

PREPARING TO WATCH

[handwritten: cucci Hermes ..., DRG ..., brada, suess]

ACTIVATING YOUR KNOWLEDGE

1 Work with a partner. Discuss the questions.

1 Can you name any fashion designers?
2 What are the most popular clothing brands at the moment?
3 What stores are famous for selling very expensive clothes?

PREDICTING CONTENT

2 Work with a partner. Look at the photos from the video and discuss the questions.

1 What is the Louis Vuitton company famous for making?
2 Who do you think shops at Louis Vuitton stores? *[handwritten: only rich people]*
3 Would you pay more for something made by a famous designer? Why or why not?

> ### GLOSSARY
>
> **branch out** (phr v) to do something that is related to what you have done in the past but that takes you in a new direction
>
> **strategy** (n) a plan that you use to achieve something
>
> **delicate** (adj) needing to be dealt with carefully in order to avoid causing trouble or offense
>
> **the masses** (n phr) the ordinary people who make up most of society
>
> **exclusive** (adj) expensive and only for people who are rich or of a high social class

WHILE WATCHING

UNDERSTANDING MAIN IDEAS

3 ▶ Watch the video. Circle the correct answers.

1 Louis Vuitton has always made products for __c__.
   a large number of people
   b stores around the world
   c the rich and famous

2 In the last 25 years, the company began making __b__ . *149*

  a expensive luggage

  b luxury clothing

  c beautiful shoes

3 Today Louis Vuitton products are sold __a__ .

  a in 40 countries

  b in more than 620 stores

  c all over the world

4 For some top customers the company will make __c__ .

  a beautiful fabrics for the masses

  b products you can walk into any store and buy

  c anything they want

5 The company sells the greatest number of items to __c__ .

  a rich people

  b Hollywood stars

  c ordinary people

4 ▶ Watch the video again. Correct the sentences.

UNDERSTANDING
DETAILS

1 A Louis Vuitton handbag can cost $150,000 and a coat can cost $50,000.
    _____ ~~5~~ ___ $15,000 _____

2 It is difficult to sell to masses of people and remain exclusive to
  other people.
    _____ delicate _____

3 You can walk into a store and buy things in the top range.
    _____ middle _____ 400 __ stores __

4 They sell very little stuff in the bottom range.
    _____ much _____

5 Owning a Louis Vuitton item shows that you can use it.
    _____ afford _____

DISCUSSION

5 Work in a small group. Discuss the questions. Then, compare your answers
  with another group.

1 What is most important to you when you buy clothes: the style, the
  cost, or the quality? What is the least important?

2 What does wearing designer clothing tell us about a person?

LISTENING

LISTENING 1

150

PREPARING TO LISTEN

UNDERSTANDING KEY VOCABULARY

1 You are going to listen to a discussion about clothes of the future. Before you listen, read the definitions. Complete the sentences with the correct form of the words in bold.

> **convert** (v) to change something into something else
> **design** (n) the way in which something is arranged or shaped
> **fabric** (n) cloth, material
> **focus on** (phr v) to give a lot of attention to one subject or thing
> **local** (adj) related to an area nearby
> **practical** (adj) suitable for the situation in which something is used
> **smart** (adj) operated by computer or digital technology
> **useless** (adj) not useful

1 Our clothes are made from 100% natural _fabric_ .
2 My _local_ shopping center has lots of great clothing stores.
3 You don't need to pack boots. We're going on a beach vacation – they'll be _useless_ !
4 Solar panels ~~change~~ _convert_ sunlight into energy.
5 _Smart_ technology, like smartphones and smart watches, allows us to be constantly connected to the Internet.
6 Those high-heeled shoes are not _practical_ for hiking up a mountain!
7 We're going to _focus on_ clothes manufacturing, rather than fashion in general.
8 I love this shirt! The _design_ is great.

USING YOUR KNOWLEDGE

2 Work in a small group. Look at the photographs. What are some topics that you think the discussion will focus on? Make a list of possible topics.

_____

_____

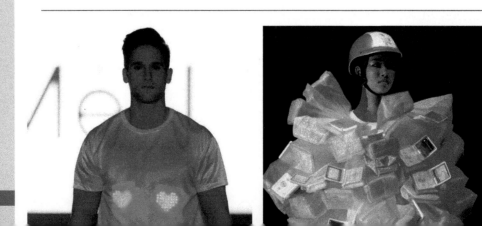

Taking notes on main ideas and details

Using an outline is an effective way to take notes while you listen. An outline helps you organize main ideas and details in a way that is easy to review later.

An outline is often organized like this:

> I Topic
>   A Main idea 1
>   1 Detail 1
>   2 Detail 2
>   3 Detail 3
>
>   B Main idea 2
>   1 Detail 1
>   2 Detail 2
>   3 Detail 3

3 ▶ 7.1 Listen to the discussion and complete the outline.

TAKING NOTES ON
MAIN IDEAS

PRISM Online Workbook

I Fashion of the (1) *Future*

  A Eco-clothes

  good for the (2) *community* but also

  (3) *environmentally* friendly

  not made by people working in bad (4) *conditions*

  collect (5) *energy* when you move the energy

  energy converted into (6) *electricity*

  B (7) *Smart* fabrics

  can (8) *kill* bacteria

  can regulate body (9) *temperature*

  can make (10) *sports* clothing to help people

  exercise in hot or cold climates

  can reduce muscle aches and prevent us from getting

  (11) *sick*

  C Designers used (12) *lights* in clothes

  (13) *dress* made from lights

  change (14) *color* as you move

152

4 ▶ 7.1 Listen to the discussion again. Write the adjective(s) the students use to describe each type of future clothing and their opinions.

type of clothing	adjective(s)	speaker's opinion (P = positive, N = negative)
eco-clothes		P
fabrics that regulate body temperature	help sports people in climet ghenge	P)
fabrics that prevent people from getting sick		N
dress made of lights	not very _____	N

POST-LISTENING

Auxiliary verbs for emphasis

In fluent speech, speakers usually contract auxiliary verbs (am → 'm, have → 've, etc.). However, to emphasize a point, they sometimes use the full form and stress the auxiliary verb.

That's interesting.
That **is** interesting. (= emphasizes that *that* is interesting)

Speakers sometimes add *do* or *does* to an affirmative sentence to emphasize a point.

I like it.
I **do** like it. (= emphasizes that I like something or suggests that the listener didn't expect me to like it.)

5 ▶ 7.2 Listen to the sentence pairs below. Underline the stressed word in each sentence.

1 a I've been reading about fashion of the future.
   b I have been reading about fashion of the future.
2 a That's amazing.
   b That is amazing.
3 a I agree that it's not very practical.
   b I do agree that it's not very practical.
4 a I think it'll be interesting.
   b I do think it'll be interesting.

6 Change the sentences to <u>emphasize</u> the words in bold by adding *do* or *does*.

1 I **believe** they can be used to make sports clothing.

I do believe...

2 It **seems** we have a lot of ideas for the future of fashion.

It does seem we have...

3 I **agree**.

I do agree

4 I **like** the idea of clothes that help people with health problems.

I do like the idea of...

5 She **buys** a lot of clothes.

She does buy a lot of clothes.

PRONUNCIATION FOR LISTENING

Vowel omission

Speakers don't always pronounce every letter in a word. Unstressed vowels are sometimes not pronounced when they appear between a consonant and /l/ or /r/.

Every is usually pronounced /ˈev·ri/.

Family is often pronounced /ˈfæm·li/.

Common words in which a vowel is often omitted

typically	favorite	different
family	average	camera
basically	every	temperature
finally	several	natural
chocolate	interesting	general

7 ▶ 7.3 Listen to the excerpts. For the words in bold, circle the vowels that are not pronounced.

1 I've been looking for an **interesting** topic, but to be honest, I haven't come up with anything yet.

2 And eco-friendly clothing **typically** helps protect the environment, too.

3 Well, these fabrics keep your body **temperature** the same in any kind of weather.

4 Anyway, it looks like we've **finally** come up with some good ideas.

5 There are a lot of **different** articles on the topic.

8 ▶ 7.3 Listen to the excerpts again. Practice saying the sentences in Exercise 7.

PRISM Online Workbook

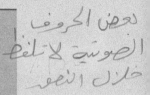

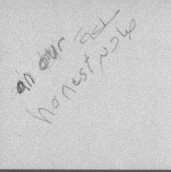

an our (handwritten) *honest نجلا*

DISCUSSION

9 Work with a partner. Discuss the questions.

154 *(handwritten)*

1 What do you think fashion in the future will be like? ✗ — *No because very Expensive (handwritten)*
2 Do you usually buy the latest fashion? Why or why not?
3 Why do some people feel it's important to be fashionable? — *Because th love change (handwritten)*

◎ LANGUAGE DEVELOPMENT

IDIOMS

LANGUAGE

> Idioms are expressions that are often used in spoken English. An idiom doesn't always have a literal meaning. It has a meaning that can't easily be understood from looking at its individual words. You need to look at the whole expression to understand it.
>
> *Hot on the heels of her fashion week show …*
> (= *close behind or straight after something* – not *having hot feet/shoes*)

PRISM **Online** Workbook

1 Look at the excerpts. What is the meaning of the expressions in bold?

1 I've been looking for an interesting topic, but to be honest, I haven't come up with anything yet. Can you **give me a hand**?
   Meaning: ___ *Can you help me* ___

2 I'm not **crazy about** that idea, to be honest.
   Meaning: *I'm not so exited about ...*

3 I don't think there are many people **dying to** wear a dress made of lights.
   Meaning: ___ *really wantto* ___

4 Aysha's new collection is **all the rage** in Doha.
   Meaning: ___ *is in every where* ___

5 She **turned** the **heads** of the fashion world with her unique designs.
   Meaning: *she caught the attention*

6 It's a **hot topic** at the moment, but I think there's a lot of misunderstanding about Muslim clothes.
   Meaning: ___ *so interesting* ___

7 Your designs are **must-haves** for Muslim women outside the United States as well.
   Meaning: ___ *important* ___

2 Match the phrases in bold in Exercise 1 with the synonyms.

a very popular ___4___

b essential ___7___

c very enthusiastic about ___2___

d got the attention ___5___

e help me ___1___

f extremely eager to ___3___

g popular talking point ___6___

PREDICTIONS AND EXPECTATIONS ABOUT THE FUTURE

There are several ways to talk about your predictions and expectations about the future.

be going to

It's about future fabrics and how we're **going to use** them.

will

In the future, we'll probably **wear** clothes that can regulate body temperature.

Future progressive

The future progressive describes an action that will be in progress at a specific time in the future. Form the future progressive with *will* or *be going to* + *be* + verb + *-ing*. So, a few years from now, we'll probably **be using** this fabric to charge our phones, right?

In the future, we're **going to be wearing** clothes that regulate our temperature.

PRISM Online Workbook

3 Complete the sentences with the future progressive form of the verbs in parentheses.

1 Now 3D printers can print clothes. In a few years, maybe people ___will printing___ (print) most of their clothes instead of shopping for them.

2 I think that in 25 years, we ___are going to wear___ (wear) clothes that keep us healthy. We'll never get sick!

3 Ten years from now, people probably ___will not useing___ (not use) laptops, tablets, or phones. We ___are not going to do___ (do) all our computing with wearable technology.

4 My friend Adam is the CEO of a successful company that develops eco-clothes. In a few years, it's likely that he ___will be making___ (make) millions of dollars. I expect he _____ (live) in a mansion!

4 Complete the sentences to make predictions about the future. Use each future form (*will*, *be going to*, future progressive) at least once. You can write about the topics in the box or other topics.

> cars   communication   fashion   homes   science   space travel   technology   the environment   your life

1 Ten years from now, _Everythink will be ~~technology~~ operating_
   I with my family
2 By the time I'm 80, _we will probably be travelling_
   to the space the
3 A hundred years from now, _Aliens from the outside of the_
   world communicating with us
4 In the year 3000, _we will be drive flying cars_

LISTENING 2

PREPARING TO LISTEN

UNDERSTANDING
KEY VOCABULARY

PRISM Online Workbook

1 You are going to listen to an interview with a fashion designer. Before you listen, read the sentences. Complete the definitions with the correct form of the words in bold.

1 Aysha's **collection** was presented during the last Fashion Week in Doha.
2 I have always tried to **combine** my culture with fashion.
3 As a teenager, I would make my own skirts and scarves. I wanted my designs to be **individual**. They were **unique**, and eventually, people **admired** my clothes rather than laughed at me.
4 Many traditional clothing **styles** are being reused by young designers.
5 My philosophy is to create clothes that are **modest**, but at the same time, give women **confidence**.

a ___3-c___ (v) to respect or approve of something
b ___5-a___ (adj) not showing too much of a person's body
c ___3-b___ (adj) different from everyone or everything else
d ___1___ (n) a selection of clothing designs that are sold at particular times of the year
e ___3-a___ (adj) considered as one thing, not part of a group
f ___2___ (v) to mix or join things together
g ___5-b___ (n) a feeling of being certain about yourself and your abilities
h ___4___ (n) ways of designing hair, clothes, furniture, etc.

2 Work with a partner. Discuss the questions.   *157*

1 What does the word *fashion* mean to you?

2 Does fashion allow people to show their personality or does it make people look and act the same?

3 Do you like the clothes in the photograph? Why or why not? *it showes their cultor*

WHILE LISTENING

3 ▶ 7.4 Listen to the first part of the interview. Answer the questions.

1 Who is Aysha Al-Husaini? *Islamic clothesdesigner*

2 Where is she from? *Qatar*

3 What is she famous for? *designing fashion*

و شبیں

ما ح
مید

4 ▶ **7.5** Listen to the second part of the interview and complete the outline. Listen for the interviewer's questions to help identify the main ideas.

I Muslim (1) _clothes_

   A Feelings about (2) _growing up in new york_

     (3) _____

     (4) _____

     (5) _____

   B Misunderstandings about (6) _muslem clothes_

     (7) _____

     (8) _____

     (9) _____ _that_ _____

   C Aysha's fashion

     (10) _____ _modest solthos give_

     (11) _____ _women conredence_

     (12) _____

     (13) _____ _shaw_ __ _cultur roots_

     (14) _____

5 ▶ **7.6** Listen to the interview again. Write *T* (true), *F* (false), or *DNS* (does not say) next to the statements. Correct the false statements.

  F   **1** Aysha grew up in Doha.   _New York_

  T   **2** It can be difficult to buy long-sleeved clothes in New York.

  T   **3** Aysha started making clothes when she was a teenager.

  F   **4** Most Muslim women wear a *burka*.   _No_

  T   **5** Aysha's teachers asked her why she didn't design Western styles of clothing.

  T   **6** Aysha's designs are for women who like to be modest.

  T   **7** Many Muslim women want to wear fashionable clothes.

  F   **8** Chinese and Indian designers don't use traditional designs.

  F   **9** You can buy Aysha's collection in Malaysia and Singapore.

POST-LISTENING

159

6 Look at your notes from the interview and answer the questions. Make notes on the parts of the interview that tell you the answer.

1 Does the fashion world respect Aysha's work? Yes

_____

2 Did Aysha enjoy growing up in New York? No didn't
She had a lot of peroblem to dress in modest

3 Do non-Muslim people understand what Muslim fashion is? No
don't understand

4 Was becoming a fashion designer easy for Aysha? No

_____

5 Is Aysha's fashion company successful? Yes it is

_____

DISCUSSION

7 Work in a small group. Think about Listening 1 and Listening 2 and answer the questions.

أمراً

1 What are some different purposes of clothing design and fashion? What purpose(s) do eco-friendly clothes achieve? What purpose(s) do Aysha Al-Husaini's fashions achieve? أهمية   القضايا
7-1 → النظام الخاص
2 Do you think it's possible to combine fashion with tradition? Why or why not? Yes

3 Aysha says that her clothes "give women confidence." Do you agree that clothes can influence how people feel about themselves? Why or why not? Yes because it caries their culturs.

4 Do you think it's better to dress in an individual way, or to dress in a similar way to everyone else? Why?
4 because not everyone has the same needs

SPEAKING

CRITICAL THINKING

At the end of this unit, you will do the Speaking Task below.

> Take part in an interview to find out attitudes about uniforms and dress codes.

SKILLS

Writing a purpose statement

Before interviewing someone, it is helpful to write a purpose statement – that is, a sentence about what you want to learn from the interview. A good purpose statement:

- is just one sentence.
- states the goal of the interview.
- uses qualitative words (*explore, understand, discover, learn about*).

The purpose of the interview is to learn how fashions have changed in the last five years, and to explore fashion trends of the next decade.

▲ ANALYZE

1 Look at your outline from Listening 2 on page 158. Then, check the best purpose statement for the interview with Aysha Al-Husaini in the list below. Why do you think it is best? What is wrong with the other statements?

1 The purpose of the interview is to explore fashions from around the world. ☐

2 The purpose of the interview is to find out about Aysha Al-Husaini's background and why she got into fashion design. In addition, I plan to learn about Muslim fashion and about Aysha's plans for her business. ☑

3 The purpose of the interview is to learn about Aysha Al-Husaini's career as a fashion designer and her chic yet traditional Muslim fashions. ☐

▲ UNDERSTAND

2 Work in a small group. Discuss the questions.

1 What is a dress code? *What we have to wear when we are there*

2 Why do some schools, colleges, and companies have a dress code? *to look profitional*

3 Look at the Speaking Task. Write a purpose statement for your interview.

▲ APPLY

My purpose statement: _____

_____

Writing good interview questions

In order to get interesting and relevant information from an interview, you need to ask good questions.

Good interview questions have these characteristics:

1 **They are open.** *Open questions* allow many possible answers. *Closed questions* limit the possible answers.

   Closed questions:

   Do you prefer the fashions of a decade ago or of today? (Answer choices: *a decade ago / today*)
   Are you interested in fashion? (Answer choices: *yes / no*)

   Open questions:

   What decade do you think had the most interesting fashions?
   How did you become interested in fashion?

2 **They are not biased.** Biased questions encourage the interviewee to answer in a certain way.

   Biased question: Don't you think fashions have gotten less attractive in the last five years? (Encourages a *yes* answer)

   Unbiased question: What's your opinion of how fashion has changed in the last five years? (Doesn't encourage a particular answer)

3 **They only have one part.** Two-part questions can confuse the interviewee. After they answer the first part, they might forget what the second part was.

   Two-part question: What is your opinion of how fashions have changed in the past five years, and what do you think of today's fashions?

   One-part question: What do you think of today's fashions?

4 **They are focused.** Focused questions make it clear what type of answer you're looking for.

   Unfocused question: What do you think about the future? (It's not clear what aspect of the future you want to know about.)

   Focused question: What do you think fashions will be like in the future?

5 **They relate to your purpose.**

   Purpose: The purpose of the interview is to explore the future of fashion.

   Unrelated question: Who is your favorite fashion designer? (This doesn't relate to the future of fashion.)

   Related question: How do you think fashion will change in the next ten years?

162

ANALYZE

4 Read the purpose statement and the interview questions. What is wrong with each question? Match the problems to the questions.

Purpose statement: The purpose of the interview is to learn about the fashions of the 1950s.

1 How did you become interested in 1950s fashion, and when did you start researching it? _C_
2 Do you like 1950s fashions? _a_
3 What do you think of the movies from the 1950s? _e_
4 What do you think of fashion? _d_
5 Don't you think that the fashions of the 1950s were boring? _b_

a closed   d unfocused
b biased   e doesn't relate to the purpose
c two-part

APPLY

5 Work in a small group. Make a list of possible questions for your interview.

1) Why you start researching about 1950s fashion?

2) Do you prefare to live at that time?

3) What would you change if you were living in 1950s

EVALUATE

6 From your list, choose five questions you would like to ask.

1 _____
2 _____
3 _____
4 _____
5 _____

ASKING FOR OPINIONS AND CHECKING INFORMATION

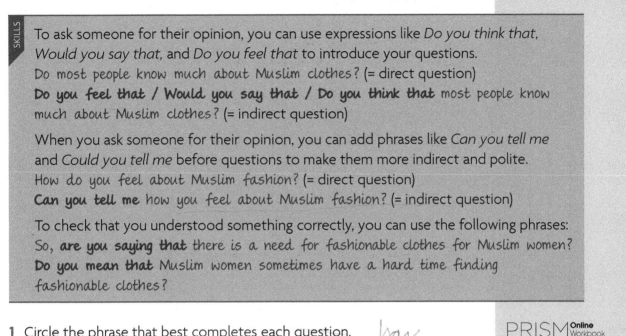

SKILLS

To ask someone for their opinion, you can use expressions like *Do you think that*, *Would you say that,* and *Do you feel that* to introduce your questions.

Do most people know much about Muslim clothes? (= direct question)

Do you feel that / Would you say that / Do you think that most people know much about Muslim clothes? (= indirect question)

When you ask someone for their opinion, you can add phrases like *Can you tell me* and *Could you tell me* before questions to make them more indirect and polite.

How do you feel about Muslim fashion? (= direct question)

Can you tell me how you feel about Muslim fashion? (= indirect question)

To check that you understood something correctly, you can use the following phrases:

So, **are you saying that** there is a need for fashionable clothes for Muslim women?

Do you mean that Muslim women sometimes have a hard time finding fashionable clothes?

PRISM Online Workbook

1 Circle the phrase that best completes each question. *han*

1 *Can you tell me / Are you saying that* it's important to educate people about Muslim fashion?

2 *Do you mean that / How do you feel about* the idea of opening stores in Singapore and Malaysia?

3 *Would you say that / Could you tell me* many women are looking for modest clothes?

4 *Are you saying that / Can you tell me* how you feel about Muslim fashion?

2 Replace each direct question with an indirect question to make it more polite or to check information.

A: *What is the best way to dress for a job interview?*

(1) _do you think_ ?

B: I think you should wear a suit and a tie.

A: *Should I wear a suit even if I don't usually wear one?*

(2) _Do you feel that_ ?

B: Yes, absolutely. As I see it, you only have 30 minutes to impress your future boss at the interview. You should look your best.

A: I'm not sure I agree. *Are my skills less important than what I look like?*

(3) _are you seen that my skills less_ ?

B: No, I'm just saying that you should dress appropriately. *Are you really going to wear jeans and a T-shirt to your job interview?*

(4) _do you mean that you wear jeans_ ?

A: I think so. The company I want to work for isn't interested in appearances.

164

SKILLS

Asking follow-up questions is a useful interviewing strategy. If a person you are interviewing says something that you find interesting and you want to know more, you can ask follow-up questions to get more information about the topic. To ask follow-up questions, use phrases like:

Can you explain why you decided to design fashions for Muslim women?

Why do you think that there is so much misunderstanding about Muslim clothes?

What do you mean by "traditional chic"?

You mentioned that when you were a teenager, your friends thought you dressed strangely in the summer. **How did you feel about that?**

Could you expand on that point?

Can you tell me more about your plans to open stores in more cities?

PRISM Online Workbook

3 Work in a small group. Take turns giving opinions on some of the topics. As you listen to the other students, ask them follow-up questions.

- People should dress up for work every day.
- High school students should wear uniforms to school.
- It's important to have an individual style and not to dress like everyone else.
- You should always look your best, even when you're just going out for coffee or to the grocery store.

SPEAKING TASK

PRISM Online Workbook

Take part in an interview to find out attitudes about uniforms and dress codes.

PREPARE

1 Look at the purpose statement and questions you created in Exercises 3 and 6 in Critical Thinking. Review your notes and add any new information.

2 Make your questions more polite. You can use language like this: *165*

Can you tell me ...   Would you say that ...
Could you tell me ...   Do you feel that ...
Do you think that ...

3 Look at your questions from the Critical Thinking section. Are they in an order that makes sense? If not, change the order so it does make sense.

4 Refer to the Task Checklist below as you prepare for your interview.

TASK CHECKLIST	✔
Ask questions in an order that makes sense.	
Clearly and politely ask for opinions.	
Check information where necessary.	
Ask follow-up questions.	

PRACTICE

5 Work with a partner. Practice your interview questions. Take notes on your partner's questions and how they could improve their interview.

6 Give each other feedback about your performance.

   1 Were there enough questions? What other questions could you add?
   2 Did the interviewer check information?
   3 Did the student give clear opinions?

7 Make improvements to your questions based on your partner's feedback.

PRESENT

8 Work with a different partner. Interview your partner. Then, be interviewed by your partner.

ON CAMPUS

PLANNING ASSIGNMENTS

PREPARING TO LISTEN

1 You are going to listen to two students planning their research project. Before you listen, check the statements that are often true for you.

1 I turn in assignments on time. ☐
2 I work on assignments at the last minute. ☐
3 It is difficult for me to begin an assignment. ☐
4 I start an assignment on time, but give up in the middle. ☐
5 I plan how I will organize my time. ☐
6 I feel overwhelmed by all the work that I have to do. ☐

2 Work in a small group and compare your answers. Why do you think it is difficult for some students to finish assignments on time?

WHILE LISTENING

3 ▶ 7.7 Listen to the two students planning their research project. When will they have their next meeting? _____

4 ▶ 7.7 Listen to the two students again. Complete the planner.

Wednesday March 1 (Today)	First meeting: plan schedule (1) _____
Thursday March 2 – Sunday March 5	(2) _____ _____
Monday March 6	Second meeting: (3) _____
Tuesday March 7	
Wednesday March 8	CLASS: OUTLINE DUE (4) _____

Planning assignments

Divide longer assignments and research projects into shorter steps. Decide when you will complete each step, and think about how much time you will need for each one. Use a planner to organize your time.

PRACTICE

5 Work with a partner. Read Clara's to-do list for the presentation. Add the tasks to the planner.

TO DO:
- agree who will present which part
- plan what to say
- practice with partner: time it!!
- get visuals: slides, photographs etc.
- prepare presentation slides together
- put main points on index cards

Wednesday March 8	Third meeting:
Thursday March 9 – Sunday March 12	
Monday March 13	Fourth meeting:
Tuesday March 14	
Wednesday March 15	PRESENTATION IN CLASS

REAL-WORLD APPLICATION

6 Work with a partner. Choose one of the assignments below. Imagine that the due date is two weeks from today. Analyze the steps involved in each assignment. Decide when you will complete each step, and when you will meet. Make a schedule for the next two weeks.

Survey

Design a survey to find out people's attitudes toward wearing uniforms at school. Ask at least ten people. Collect your results and present them to the class.

Research and Presentation

Prepare a 5-minute presentation about an important fashion designer. Include pictures with your presentation.

Video

Make a 1–2 minute video about students' fashion choices at your school. Include interviews with three students.

LEARNING OBJECTIVES

Listening skill	Understand paraphrases
Pronunciation	Silent letters
Speaking skills	Use gerunds as subjects to talk about actions; present reasons and evidence to support an argument; use paraphrases
Speaking Task	Take part in a discussion about whether young people should be allowed to have credit cards
On Campus	Meet with your academic advisor

ACTIVATE YOUR KNOWLEDGE

Work with a partner. Discuss the questions.

1 What can young people do in your country to earn money?
2 How do you save money?
3 Is it worth spending money on things like designer clothes and expensive cars?

WATCH AND LISTEN

PREPARING TO WATCH

ACTIVATING YOUR KNOWLEDGE

1 Work with a partner. Discuss the questions.

1 What companies were started by one or two people?
2 Do you think most people need a lot of money to start a business? Why or why not?
3 What types of expensive equipment might someone need to buy when they start a business?

PREDICTING CONTENT USING VISUALS

2 Work with a partner. Look at the photos from the video and discuss the questions.

1 What do you think TechShop is?
2 What kinds of things do you think people make with these machines?
3 Do you think the man in the suit works for TechShop? What could his job be?

GLOSSARY

get laid off (phr v) to lose one's job, usually because there is no work for the person to do

prototype (n) the first model or example of something new that can be developed or copied in the future

entrepreneur (n) someone who starts a business, especially when this involves risk

machinery (n) machines, often large ones in a factory

partnership (n) the joining of two people or organizations to work together to achieve something

expand (v) to increase in size or amount, or to cause to do this

---

WHILE WATCHING

3 ▶ Watch the video. Fill in the blanks to complete the sentences.

UNDERSTANDING
MAIN IDEAS

1 TechShop offers people access to expensive _____ .
2 The entrepreneurs create prototypes of _____ they hope to sell.
3 The woman is making products for _____ .
4 One man has designed a special __iped__ cover.
5 Another man has created a way to make _____ cooler.
6 TechShop is expanding to more _____ .

4 ▶ Watch again. Write *T* (true), *F* (false), or *DNS* (does not say) next to the statements. Then, correct the false statements.

UNDERSTANDING
DETAILS

_T_ 1 TechShop attracts people who like to work for others.

_____

_F_ 2 People usually work in small groups at TechShop.

_____

_F_ 3 Most people at TechShop like to buy things.

_____

_F_ 4 Some of the inventors are now selling their products on the street.

_____

_T_ 5 One man has hired 30 people.

_____

_F_ 6 The success of TechShop shows that many people with a lot of money have great ideas.

_____

DISCUSSION

5 Work in a small group. Discuss the questions. Then, compare your answers with another group.

1 What are three differences between working for a small company (1–50 people) and a large company (50+ people)?
2 Would you like to own your own business? Why or why not?
3 If you started a business, what kind of business would it be?

LISTENING

PREPARING TO LISTEN

**UNDERSTANDING
KEY VOCABULARY**

1 You are going to listen to a radio program about millionaire lifestyles. Before you listen, circle the best definition for the word or phrase in bold.

1 If you want to **save money**, you could stop eating out in expensive restaurants.

   a to lose money quickly
   (b) to keep money to use in the future

2 I just paid my college tuition. That's why I can't **afford** to go out this weekend.

   a to want to do something
   (b) to have enough money to buy or do something

3 Sarah took out a big **loan** to buy her first house.

   (a) an amount of money that you borrow and have to pay back
   b a credit card

4 He used his credit card to go on vacation. Now he has a huge **debt**.

   a a suitcase
   (b) money that is owed to someone else

5 My cousin is a **millionaire**. He has three houses and four cars, and he goes on exotic vacations every year.

   (a) a person who has more than 1,000,000 dollars
   b a person who likes to travel

6 I borrowed money to buy my car. Every month I have to make a $300 **payment**.

   a a credit card
   (b) an amount of money paid

7 Marta puts 10% of every paycheck into the bank. Now she has $15,000 in **savings**.

   (a) money you keep, usually in a bank
   b money you spend every month

**USING YOUR
KNOWLEDGE**

2 Work with a partner. Discuss the questions.

1 What kinds of cars do you think millionaires drive?
2 What kinds of houses do they live in?
3 What kinds of clothes do they wear?

3 ▶ 8.1 Look at the book cover and listen to the introduction to a radio program about millionaire lifestyles. Discuss the questions.

1 The speaker says that the results of the study were surprising. Can you guess why they were surprising?
2 What does *wealthy* mean?
3 What do you think the rest of the program will be about?

THE SECRET OF BEING WEALTHY

مليونير
ثري
غني

WHILE LISTENING

4 Work in a small group. Check the behaviors of millionaires that you think are true.

LISTENING FOR MAIN IDEAS

Millionaires ...
1 drive luxury cars and eat in expensive restaurants. ☑
2 know how much money they spend on food, clothes, etc. ☒
3 live in the same place for a long time. ☑
4 don't spend a lot of money on cars. ☑
5 have successful relationships. ☑
6 borrow money from the bank. ☒
7 are happy with what they have. ☑
8 buy expensive things to feel better. ☒

5 ▶ 8.2 Listen to the radio program and underline the behaviors in Exercise 4 that it says are true of millionaires.

6 ▶ 8.2 Listen to the radio program again. Complete the notes with numbers and percentages.

TAKING NOTES ON DETAILS

(1)_____ % of millionaires know how much they spend every year.

(2)___½___ % of millionaires have lived in the same house for over (3)___20___ years.

About (4)___65___ % of millionaires live in homes that cost (5)__350,000__ or less.

(6)___86___ % of luxury cars are owned by people who can't afford them.

POST-LISTENING

Understanding paraphrases

To help listeners understand what they're saying, speakers sometimes paraphrase. That is, they explain an idea in different words, often in a simpler or shorter way. To recognize paraphrases, listen for the phrases in bold, which often introduce paraphrases.

Most people think that rich people live <u>lavish lifestyles</u> – **that is**, they <u>drive very expensive cars, eat in expensive restaurants, own a yacht, or live in big houses</u>.

Millionaires are often <u>financially savvy</u>. **To put it another way**, they're <u>smart about how to save and spend money</u>.

Most millionaires actually seem to have <u>ordinary lifestyles</u>. **In other words**, <u>they have normal cars, average houses, and so on</u>.

Sometimes speakers paraphrase without using an introductory phrase.

John Holm decided to <u>study the behavior of wealthy people</u>. He <u>paid close attention to what rich people do</u>.

7 Read the sentences. Underline the words or phrases in each sentence that mean the same thing.

   1 The important lesson here is to live within your means – that is, don't spend more money than you have.

   2 Instead, they have spent all their money trying to show off – showing other people that they might be wealthy.

   3 Even though Liz is a millionaire, she's very frugal. In other words, she's careful about where she spends her money.

   4 When I was growing up, my family was economically disadvantaged. To put it another way, we didn't have much money.

PRONUNCIATION FOR LISTENING

Silent letters

Some English words include letters that are not pronounced. This is because the pronunciation of the words has changed over time, but the spelling has stayed the same. For example, the letter *w* is not pronounced in *write* and the letter *b* is not pronounced in *comb*. There aren't any rules about which letters are silent and which aren't – you just have to learn them.

8 ▶ **8.3** Listen to the sentences. Pay attention to the pronunciation of the words in bold. Circle the letters that are not pronounced.

1 Most people think that rich people live lavish lifestyles, that is they drive very expensive cars, eat in expensive restaurants, own a **yacht**, or live in big houses.

2 In other words, having expensive things is not always a **sign** that someone is rich.

3 On the other hand, people who look rich – the people who drive the latest Ferrari or only wear **designer** clothes – may not actually be rich at all.

4 As a result, they don't spend too much, and they don't get into **debt**.

5 There is no **doubt** that it's more difficult to save money if you are single.

6 So, what can we learn from the wealthy? The **answer** is surprisingly simple.

9 Work with a partner. Take turns saying the sentences in Exercise 8.

DISCUSSION

10 Work alone. Decide if you agree with the points made in the program. Make notes to explain why or why not and think of examples from your own life.

1 Pay close attention to your money.
2 Don't spend more than you have.
3 Don't try to look rich.
4 Pay close attention to your relationships.
5 Be happy with what you have.

11 Work in a small group and share your ideas. Decide together which lesson you think is the most important and why.

COLLOCATIONS WITH *PAY* AND *MONEY*

1 Read the definitions. Complete the sentences with the correct form of the words in bold.

> **borrow money** (v phr) to take money and promise to pay it back later
> **lose money** (v phr) to have less money than you had before
> **make money** (v phr) to earn money
> **owe money** (v phr) to have to pay someone money that you borrowed
> **pay a fine** (v phr) to pay money as a punishment for not obeying a rule or law
> **pay in cash** (v phr) to pay for something with money (not a credit card)
> **pay off** (v phr) to pay all of the money that you owe
> **raise money** (v phr) to collect money from other people, often for charity
> **save money** (v phr) to keep money for use in the future
> **spend money** (v phr) to give money as a payment for something

1 My company didn't ___make money___ last quarter. Our new products haven't been selling well.

2 I never use a credit card. I always ___pay in cash___.

3 If you have a lot of debt, it's a good idea to ___pay off___ your loans a little bit every month.

4 Peter had to ___pay a fine___ for parking in an illegal place.

5 Investing in the stock market is risky. If you're not lucky, you might ___lose money___.

6 My brother is going to ___borrow mon e___from my parents so he can buy a new car.

7 We want to ___save money___ for our wedding, so we have to reduce our spending.

8 I ___owe money___ to my cousin. She lent me $20 for gas last weekend.

9 The soccer team is trying to ___raise money___ to buy new uniforms.

10 Maria isn't going on vacation with us because she doesn't want to ___spend money___. She should get a job that pays more!

PRESENT AND FUTURE REAL CONDITIONALS

LANGUAGE

Use present real conditionals to talk about general facts, truths, and habits. Use *if* + simple present in the *if* clause. Use the simple present in the main clause.

if + simple present

If people **have** a lot of money, they **are** happier.

simple present

Use future real conditionals to talk about things that are possible now or in the future, and their likely results. Use *if* + simple present in the *if* clause and a future verb form in the main clause.

if + simple present

If I **win** the lottery, I **will buy** a new car.

future verb form

You can also use present and future real conditionals to give advice and suggestions. These are formed with *if you* ... in the *if* clause and an imperative in the main clause.

If **you** want to be rich, **save** a lot of money!

imperative

PRISM Online Workbook

2 Look at the statements. Write *A* next to the sentences that give advice or make a suggestion and *T* next to the sentences that talk about things that are generally true or possible.

1 If you want to be a millionaire, don't spend a lot on your house. ___ A

2 If you don't have to worry about monthly credit card payments, you're less likely to buy things to make you feel better. ___ T

3 If you change houses a lot and live in expensive places, it will be impossible to save money. ___ T

4 If you want to comment on these ideas, go to our website. ___ A

3 These sentences include mistakes. Delete or change one word in each sentence to make it correct.

1 If you want to spend money, ~~you~~ don't buy lots of expensive things.

_____

2 If you have time, ~~listened~~ to this radio program.

_____

3 If I have money, I always ~~bought~~ buy new clothes.

_____

4 If you ~~will~~ pay off all your debts, you will be happier.

_____

4 Complete the sentences with your own ideas. Then, work with a partner and discuss your sentences.

1 If you want to save money, _____ dont spend a lot on your house _____ .
2 If you want to be rich, _____ save a lot money _____ .
3 If you want to get a better job, _____ .
4 If you wear expensive clothes, _____ .

LISTENING 2

PREPARING TO LISTEN

1 You are going to listen to a discussion about being paid for getting good grades in college. Before you listen, read the definitions. Complete the sentences with the correct form of the words in bold.

UNDERSTANDING
KEY VOCABULARY

PRISM Online
Workbook

decision (n) a choice that someone makes after thinking about the options
encourage (v) to make someone more likely to do something
manage (v) to control or organize something or someone
minimum wage (n) the lowest pay for an hour's work that a worker can be legally paid
responsible (adj) showing good judgment and able to be trusted
sense (n) a quality of being or feeling loyal, responsible, etc.
services (n) systems that supply things that people need

1 My teacher _____ encourage _____ me to apply to college. I followed her advice, and I'm going to graduate next month!
2 Meg works at a restaurant for _____ minimum wage _____ . She doesn't make a lot of money, but it pays her rent.
3 She is a hardworking and _____ responsible _____ student. She always does her homework and gets to class on time.
4 I have trouble getting all of my work done on schedule. I need to learn to _____ manage _____ my time better.
5 Because they need to make money, many young people make the _____ decision _____ to work rather than go to college.
6 Going to college while working part-time requires a strong _____ sense _____ of responsibility.
7 My school provides many _____ services _____ , including tutoring and career counseling.

2 ▶ 8.4 Work in a small group. Listen to the introduction to the discussion and look at the question. What arguments do you think will be mentioned in the discussion? Complete the chart with arguments for and against the idea.

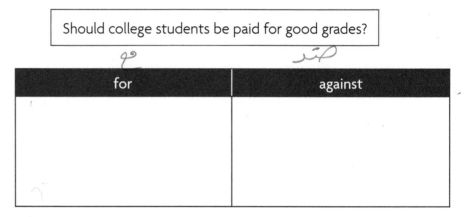

for	against

WHILE LISTENING

3 ▶ 8.5 Listen to the discussion. Write the arguments that the speakers mention in the chart. Underline the arguments that were the same as your predictions.

for	against

4 ▶ 8.6 Listen to part of the discussion again. Write the numbers you hear and what the numbers refer to.

Numbers	What they refer to
1 _____	_____
2 _____	_____
3 _____	_____
4 _____	_____

POST-LISTENING

5 Look at the excerpts from the discussion. Circle the correct answer to the question after each excerpt.

> I understand that many students drop out of college because of financial problems. ... However, will paying students really encourage them to continue?

1 The speaker thinks that ...
   a we should help students who quit school because they are poor.
   b paying students for good grades will not solve the problem.

> I can see your point, but we have already spent a lot on student services.

2 The speaker thinks ...
   a there is no point spending more on student services.
   b student services are a great way to solve the problem.

> I realize that students need encouragement to stay in school, but are we going in the right direction?

3 The speaker thinks paying students for good grades ...
   a will encourage them to stay in school.
   b might be a mistake.

6 Look again at the excerpts in Exercise 5.

- Underline the phrases that are used to show that the speaker understands the other person's point of view.
- Circle the words that are used to show that the speaker is going to give a different point of view.

DISCUSSION

7 Work in a small group. Think about Listening 1 and Listening 2 and answer the questions.

1 Which information in the listenings surprised you the most?
2 Do you think college students should be paid to go to college? How about high school? Even millionaires? Why or why not?
3 Do you think that being paid to get good grades would persuade a wealthy person to stay in college and work hard? Why or why not?
4 Do you think parents should pay their children for good grades? Why or why not?
5 What do you think most motivates people to succeed in school and at work? Money or something else?

SPEAKING

CRITICAL THINKING

At the end of this unit, you will do the Speaking Task below.

▶ Take part in a discussion about whether young people should be allowed to have credit cards.

▲ UNDERSTAND

1 Complete the chart with arguments from Listening 2. Use information from your notes on page 180.

Position: College students should be paid for good grades.

arguments that support the position	arguments that oppose the position
Argument 1: Supporting details:	Argument 1: Supporting details:
Argument 2: Supporting details:	Argument 2: Supporting details:

2 Work with a partner. Read the news story and discuss the questions.

> With the financial difficulties faced by many countries around the world, more and more banks are reaching out to teenagers and college-age students. Many young people are sent advertisements for free credit cards as soon as they become old enough. As a result, many of them get into debt and start their lives owing money. This situation has started a public discussion as to whether young people should be allowed to have credit cards.

1 Do you have a credit card? If yes, at what age did you get it?
2 If you don't have a credit card, would you like to have one? Why?
3 What are some of the problems with credit cards?
4 What is the best age to have your first credit card? Why?

3 Work alone. Make a list of the advantages and disadvantages of allowing young people to have credit cards.

EVALUATE ▲

advantages

1 _____

2 _____

3 _____

4 _____

disadvantages

1 _____

2 _____

3 _____

4 _____

4 Work with a partner and discuss your ideas from Exercise 3.

5 Work alone. Decide which side of the argument you support. Complete the chart with your three best arguments for each side. Add supporting details for each argument.

APPLY ▲

arguments that support the position	arguments that oppose the position
Argument 1: Supporting details:	Argument 1: Supporting details:
Argument 2: Supporting details:	Argument 2: Supporting details:

USING GERUNDS AS SUBJECTS TO TALK ABOUT ACTIONS

Niyu (handwritten)

LANGUAGE

The gerund is the *-ing* form of a verb. It functions as a noun and can act as the subject of a sentence. When the gerund acts as the subject of a sentence, use a singular verb form. Make a sentence negative by adding *not* before the gerund.

To focus on an action, use gerund forms in a noun phrase at the start of a sentence. Make this noun phrase the subject of the sentence and put it before the main verb.

<u>Giving</u> children money **will teach** them how to be responsible.
    gerund

<u>Not **paying** children for housework</u> **is** a bad idea as they won't learn about work.   gerund

PRISM Online Workbook

Niyal (handwritten)

1 Underline the subject in the sentences.

  1 Learning should be about studying new things and improving yourself.
  2 Saving money is not easy if you have bills to pay.
  3 Reading books about millionaires is not a good way to get rich.
  4 Teaching children about money should start at an early age.

2 Rewrite the sentences to focus more on the actions in bold.

  1 It is not a good idea to **pay children for housework.**
     Paying children for housework is not a good idea.
  2 It is very important to **teach children to save money**
     Teaching children to save money is very important.
  3 You can encourage children to study if you **pay them.**
     Paying them can encourage children to study.
  4 You can spoil children at an early age if you **give them money.**
     Giving children money can spoil them at an early age.
  5 It's difficult to **learn about money** when you're a child.
     Learning about money is difficult when you're a child.

Niyal (handwritten)

3 Work with a partner. Complete the sentences with your own ideas.

1 Teaching children about money is _____ .
2 Giving money to charity is _____ .
3 Being a millionaire is _____ .
4 Saving money is _____ .
5 Spending money on luxury cars is _____ .
6 Buying designer clothes is _____ .

PRESENTING REASONS AND EVIDENCE TO SUPPORT AN ARGUMENT

Speakers use reasons and evidence to make their argument stronger and persuade listeners to agree with them. You can use these phrases to introduce reasons and evidence:

One effect/result/consequence of being a couple is that it's easier to save money. If there are two of you, it's easier to pay attention to what money you have and what you're spending.

However, will paying students really encourage them to continue? **In my experience**, it won't.

Advisors can help students learn to manage their time better. **As a consequence / As a result / Because of that / Due to that**, students will do better in school and will be more likely to graduate.

4 Circle the correct phrase in each sentence.

1 Around 75% of millionaires know exactly how much money they have, and they know exactly how much they spend on food, bills, clothes, etc. *As a result / In my experience* , they don't spend too much, and they don't get into debt.

2 *One effect of / As a result of* paying college students would be that more students would finish their education.

3 *One consequence of / In my experience,* treating students like adults makes them more responsible.

4 *As a consequence of / Because of that* saving money, they can plan for their future.

5 Millionaires often buy houses that aren't very expensive. *Because of that, / One consequence of* they are able to save a lot of money.

USING PARAPHRASES

SKILLS

To make your arguments clearer, use paraphrases. Paraphrases can help you explain or summarize something you think your audience might not understand very well. Paraphrases also help your listeners remember the information by letting them hear it a second time.

The first important thing is that millionaires always have a good handle on their budget. **In other words**, they know how much they're spending. In John Holm's opinion, being "wealthy" is a feeling. **That is**, it doesn't mean being rich or having millions of dollars. It means being happy with what you have.

They don't spend too much, and they don't get into debt. They can plan for the future and save their money. **To sum up**, the lesson here is that you should never spend more money than you have!

PRISM **Online** Workbook

5 Complete the paraphrases. Then, read your paraphrases to a partner. Did your partner understand what you were saying?

1 I can't afford to buy a new car right now. In other words,

_____ .

2 Millionaires often have simple lifestyles. That is,

_____ .

3 So, what can we learn from the wealthy? The answer is surprisingly simple. To sum up, _____ .

4 Students need encouragement to stay in school. To put it another way,

_____ .

> Take part in a discussion about whether young people should be allowed to have credit cards.

PREPARE

1 Look at the chart you created in Exercise 5 in Critical Thinking. Review your notes and add any new information.

2 Use the Task Checklist below to prepare your point for the discussion.

TASK CHECKLIST	✔
Use collocations with *pay* and *money* correctly.	
Used conditional sentences correctly.	
Use gerunds to talk about actions clearly.	
Present reasons and evidence to support your argument.	
Use paraphrases.	

PRACTICE

3 Work in a small group. Discuss your opinions about whether young people should be allowed to have credit cards. Give your reasons and evidence.

4 Discuss the questions in your group.

   1 Was your point of view strong and well presented?
   2 What could you improve about your arguments?

DISCUSS

5 Work in different groups. Each group should have some students who agree with the topic and some who disagree. Discuss the topic.

MEETING WITH YOUR ACADEMIC ADVISOR

PREPARING TO LISTEN

1 You are going to listen to a meeting between a first-year student, Daniel, and his academic advisor. Before you listen, complete the text with the bold words from the box.

> **course catalog** (n) an official list of the courses and programs available at a university
>
> **credits** (n) values given to a course or a class. A three-credit class is longer and more demanding than a two-credit class.
>
> **general education requirements** (n) classes that all students in a university are required to take before they can graduate
>
> **major** (n) the main subject that a student studies in college
>
> **prerequisites (prereq)** (n) qualifications or classes you must complete before you can register for a higher-level class or program of study

In the second year, most students are ready to study a subject in more detail, or to declare a (1)_____ . You can find information about programs of study in the (2)_____ . You will see what classes are required for your major, and how many (3)_____ each class is worth. Find out about if there are any (4)_____ that you should have before you start your major classes. In addition, you will probably have to take some extra classes outside your major to fulfill your (5)_____ .

SKILLS

Meeting with your academic advisor

Your academic advisor helps you plan the classes that you will take in college in order to fulfill the requirements of your major. Meet with your advisor regularly, and prepare questions so that you make the best use of your advisor's time.

---

2 Look at Daniel's notes for the meeting. Write formal questions for him to ask his academic advisor, using his notes.

1 Declare major: (When?)	**5** Gen ed requirements: how many credits?
2 Take economics classes this year?	**6** Art History OK?
3 Any prereq courses?	**7** How to register? When?
4 How many credits per semester?	

WHILE LISTENING

3 ▶ 8.7 Listen to the meeting. What are the four classes that Daniel is going to take this semester?

1 _____   2 _____   3 _____   4 _____

4 ▶ 8.7 Listen to the meeting again. Write the answers to Daniel's questions in Exercise 2.

PRACTICE

5 Match the questions and the answers.

1 How long will it take to get a degree? _____
2 How many credits can I take in one semester? _____
3 What are the general education requirements? _____
4 Can I take classes during the summer? _____
5 What are the prerequisites for the nursing program? _____
6 Can I get credit for classes that I took at community college? _____
7 What classes are offered online? _____

a The university requires students to take 12 credits in science and the humanities.
b Most students take about 12 credits a semester.
c Some of the popular introductory classes are offered online.
d Yes. A lot of classes are taught during the summer session.
e Yes. You can usually get transfer credit for classes that you have already taken.
f It takes about eight semesters.
g You will need to take classes in anatomy and biology before you can enroll in nursing.

REAL-WORLD APPLICATION

6 Look online for a degree or certificate program that you are interested in. Find the answers to the following questions.

1 How long does the program take?
2 What classes are required?
3 Are there any prerequisites?
4 Does the school have general education requirements?
5 What additional questions might you ask an advisor?

7 Present the information to your class or in a small group.

GLOSSARY OF KEY VOCABULARY

Words that are part of the Academic Word List are noted with an **A** in this glossary.

UNIT 1 ANIMALS

LISTENING 1

abuse (n) violent or unfair treatment of someone

conditions (n) the situation in which someone lives or works

cruel (adj) not kind

issue (n) a topic or problem that causes concern and discussion

protect (v) to keep safe from danger

suffer (v) to feel pain or unhappiness

survive **A** (v) to continue to live, in spite of danger and difficulty

welfare (n) someone's or something's health and happiness

LISTENING 2

damage (v) to hurt

depend on (v phr) to need; to rely on

endangered (adj) at risk of no longer existing

habitat (n) the natural environment of an animal or plant

melt (v) to become liquid as a result of heating

source **A** (n) where something comes from

species (n) a group of plants or animals that shares similar features

threat (n) the possibility of trouble, danger, or disaster

UNIT 2 THE ENVIRONMENT

LISTENING 1

alternative **A** (adj) different from what is usual or traditional

crisis (n) a very dangerous or difficult situation

environmental **A** (adj) relating to the air, water and land

limited (adj) small in amount or number

provide (v) to give something

resource **A** (n) something you have and can use

solution (n) a way of solving a problem

system (n) a way of doing things

LISTENING 2

affordable (adj) not expensive

benefit **A** (n) an advantage

disaster (n) terrible accident that causes a lot of damage

long-term (adj) continuing for a long time

opponent (n) a person or group of people who disagree with an idea

pollute (v) to make something, like air or water, dirty or harmful

risk (n) the possibility of something bad happening

UNIT 3 TRANSPORTATION

LISTENING 1

avoid (v) to stay away from something

compare (v) to look for the difference between two or more things

consist of Ⓐ (v) to be made of something

crash (n) an accident in which a vehicle hits something

cure (n) something that will make a sick person healthy again

extreme (adj) very large in amount or degree

safety (n) the condition of not being in danger

scared (adj) feeling fear or worry

LISTENING 2

break the law (idm) to fail to obey the rules of a country, state or city

convenient (adj) easy to use or suiting your plans well

fine (n) money that has to be paid as a punishment for not obeying a law

injure Ⓐ (v) to hurt or cause physical harm

pass (v) to go past someone or something

prevent (v) to stop something from happening

respect (n) polite behavior towards someone

solve (v) to find a way to fix a problem

UNIT 4 CUSTOMS AND TRADITIONS

LISTENING 1

anniversary (n) the day on which an important event happened on a previous year

celebration (n) an occasion when you do something to mark a special day or event

die out (phr v) to become more rare and eventually disappear

generation Ⓐ (n) all the people of about the same age within a society or a family

interact Ⓐ (v) communicate and do things with someone/something

multicultural (adj) including people who have many different customs and beliefs

political (adj) relating to the activities of the government

social (adj) relating to a large group of people who live together in an organized way

LISTENING 2

behavior (n) a particular way of acting

commercial (adj) related to buying and selling things

event (n) anything that happens, especially something important or unusual

graduate (v) to complete school or college successfully

obligation (n) something that you have to do

occasion (n) a special event or ceremony

personal (adj) related to an individual person and not anyone else

thoughtful (adj) showing care and consideration in how you treat other people

UNIT 5 HEALTH AND FITNESS

LISTENING 1

habit (n) something that you do regularly

illness (n) a disease of the body or mind

overweight (adj) being heavier than you want or than is good for you

prove (v) to show that something is true

unhealthy (adj) not good for your health; not strong and well

work out (phr v) to exercise in order to make your body stronger

LISTENING 2

concentration Ⓐ (n) the ability to give your whole attention to one thing

mental Ⓐ (adj) relating to the mind

participate Ⓐ (v) to take part in or become involved in an activity

performance (n) how well a person does an activity

reduce (v) to make (something) less in size, amount, etc.

relax Ⓐ (v) to become less stiff, tense, tight, or worried

stress Ⓐ (n) worry caused by a difficult situation

treatment (n) something that you do to try to cure an illness or injury

UNIT 6 DISCOVERY AND INVENTION

LISTENING 1

design Ⓐ (v) to make or draw plans for something

develop (v) to make something over a period of time

device Ⓐ (n) a piece of equipment that is used for a specific purpose

diagram (n) a simple picture that shows how something works or what it looks like

discover (v) to find information, a place, or an object, especially for the first time

invent (v) to create something that had never been made before

scientific (adj) relating to the study of science

technology Ⓐ (n) knowledge, equipment, and method used in science and industry

LISTENING 2

access Ⓐ (v) to be able to enter or use something

allow (v) to make it possible for someone to do something

app (n) (*application*) software designed for a particular purpose that you can download onto a smartphone or other mobile device

create Ⓐ (v) to make something new, or invent something

industry (n) the companies and activities involved in the process of producing goods for sale

install (v) to put new software onto a computer or mobile device

product (n) something that is made to be sold

user (n) a person who uses a product, machine, or service

UNIT 7 FASHION

LISTENING 1

convert (A) (v) to change something into something else

design (A) (n) the way in which something is arranged or shaped

fabric (n) cloth, material

focus on (A) (phr v) to give a lot of attention to one subject or thing

local (adj) related to an area nearby

practical (adj) suitable for the situation in which something is used

smart (A) (adj) operated by computer or digital technology

useless (adj) not useful

LISTENING 2

admire (v) to respect or approve of something

collection (n) a selection of clothing designs that are sold at particular times of the year

combine (v) to mix or join things together

confidence (n) a feeling of being certain about yourself and your abilities

individual (A) (adj) considered as one thing, not part of a group

modest (adj) not showing too much of a person's body

style (A) (n) a way of designing hair, clothes, furniture, etc.

unique (A) (adj) different from everyone or everything else

UNIT 8 ECONOMICS

LISTENING 1

afford (v) to have enough money to buy or do something

debt (n) money that is owed to someone else

loan (n) an amount of money that you borrow and have to pay back

millionaire (n) a person who has more than 1,000,000 dollars

payment (n) an amount of money paid

save money (v phr) to keep money to use in the future

savings (n) money you keep, usually in a bank

LISTENING 2

decision (n) a choice that someone makes after thinking about the options

encourage (v) to make someone more likely to do something

manage (v) to use or organize your time or money

minimum wage (n) the lowest pay for an hour's work that a worker can be legally paid

responsible (adj) showing good judgment and able to be trusted

sense (n) a quality of being or feeling loyal, responsible, etc.

services (n) systems that supply things that people need

I couldn't catch up

UNIT 1

▶ **The Mental Skills of Chimpanzees**

Narrator: For 30 years, scientists at Georgia State University have been studying the mental skills of chimpanzees. They're finding out if chimpanzees can plan ahead and how much they plan ahead.

Man: OK, I'm going to set up the computer, right here.

Narrator: They use a computer maze to find out about the chimpanzee's ability. In the wild, chimpanzees have to find food and protect themselves, so they probably need to make plans.

But how good are they at planning?

One of the chimpanzees, named Panzee, is excellent. She can often complete difficult mazes that she's never seen before better than humans.

Man: Tell me what you want.

Narrator: This is an amazing discovery! Panzee doesn't make many mistakes, and she can sometimes see the solution to the maze faster than a human can.

The ability to look ahead and find the way from the beginning to the end of the maze means she's very smart.

And it means that planning before acting is not just a human skill.

Scientist: Chimpanzees do plan ahead. I don't believe that they can plan ahead nearly so far as we can. I think also that they reflect upon the past but not to the degree that we do. I would suggest that chimpanzees are able to plan ahead over the course of several days, whereas we can plan ahead for years or centuries if we wish.

◀))) 1.1

Host: Hello and welcome. Today's debate is on using animals for work. The first animal that was domesticated by humans is the dog.

Even now, dogs are still used to **protect** our houses and keep us safe. Other domesticated animals – used for food – include sheep, cows, and goats. The first donkeys were used by humans approximately 6,000 years ago in Egypt. Horses were domesticated 5,000 years ago in Europe and Asia. All these animals have been used to help human beings **survive**, either by providing food or by working for us. Horses, camels, elephants – they have all helped humans explore their land and transport goods from one place to another. But is this fair? What about animal rights? To argue for this **issue** today we have Amy Johnson, an animal rights activist and writer. To argue against the issue is Dr. Jacob Kuryan. Dr. Kuryan is a professor of zoology, which is the scientific study of animals, and a writer of several books on animal **welfare**. You both have two minutes to introduce your point of view. Ms. Johnson, would you like to begin?

Ms. Johnson: Thank you for inviting me to this debate. It's well known that animals have worked side by side with humans for thousands of years. In fact, they helped us develop our civilization and helped humans survive. Animals, like elephants and horses, were used to build amazing structures, like the pyramids in Egypt. Yet their hard work and suffering are hardly ever recognized. For example, horses, camels, and elephants were used to transport armies and soldiers during wars, and many of these animals died in these wars. And there are other examples. Even now, dogs are used to pull sleds in cold climates and elephants are used for logging. These animals work long hours and live in difficult **conditions**. However, they get very little reward. Humans just use them to their advantage. My main argument is that in the modern world, there is no longer any need to use animals for work. We have technology that can replace them. It's similar to using children to work in factories. Two hundred years ago, factory owners got rich by using children. Nowadays, people still get rich by using animals to do work for them. The problem is that the animals have no one to represent them and protect their rights. Even though animals work hard for us, they are often abandoned when they get sick or too old to work. They **suffer**. In short, I strongly believe that using animals for work is an old-fashioned and **cruel** practice.

Host: Thank you, Ms. Johnson. Dr. Kuryan – your introduction, please.

Dr. Kuryan: Thank you. It's true that animals have helped our civilization develop. Camels and horses helped us carry goods across huge distances. Dogs helped us hunt and protected us from wild animals. Humans don't have the skills or strength to do these jobs. I want to argue that, in many developing countries, poor people still need animals to survive. These are people who can't afford cars, house alarms, or expensive machines. Another point is that not all animal use is **abuse**. On the contrary, without humans, these domesticated animals would not have been able to survive. They need us to take care of them. There are many animal lovers around the world who work in animal shelters and help animals. There are laws that stop animal suffering. And people give a lot of money to animal charities and organizations that help save wildlife. At the same time, there are still millions of children in the world who don't get this kind of treatment. They go without food or clothing. I strongly believe that, in a modern society, people often care more about animals than they do about poor people.

Host: Thank you both for your arguments! Now, let's hear from our listeners …

🔊 1.2

Hello, I'd like to thank you all for coming. I know that you're all busy students, and I appreciate that you've taken the time to be here today.

So, what do you think of when you hear the words *climate change* and *global warming*?

If you're like most people, you think about warmer temperatures, floods, droughts, huge storms … and maybe polar bears. That's what I'm going to talk about today – the polar bear and the human **threats** to this beautiful, powerful, majestic animal.

It's widely known that polar bears are now an **endangered species**. There are only about 26,000 polar bears in the world today, and it's believed that most of them will be gone by 2050 if nothing changes. There are several threats to polar bears, and all of them are due to climate change.

The biggest threat is the loss of sea ice **habitat**. Climate change **damages** the sea ice that polar bears **depend on** for survival. Every summer the ice **melts** and it freezes again in winter, but rising ocean temperatures mean that the ice stays melted for longer periods each year, and when it does freeze, there's less and less of it.

The disappearing ice has several negative effects. For example, it makes it difficult for polar bears to search for seals, their main **source** of food. Polar bears need to stand on ice to hunt for seals. So when there isn't enough ice, they become hungry, and can even die from lack of food.

A second threat is contact between humans and polar bears. When there is less sea ice, polar bears have to spend more time on land. This results in more contact with humans. When polar bears go near towns, people sometimes kill the bears to protect themselves.

A third human threat to polar bears is industrial development, such as oil production and shipping. As the ice disappears, the ocean is growing. This means there may be more oil production in the Arctic, and the threat of oil spills could increase. Contact with oil will kill polar bears. And the oil business will bring more ships to the Arctic, which are dangerous to polar bears.

However, there is good news: it may not be too late to save the polar bear. Here's what people are already doing.

First, Arctic communities are trying to reduce contact between humans and polar bears. More lights in public places, electric fences, and warning plans when bears enter towns all help to protect polar bears from humans, and humans from polar bears.

Second, governments have made laws that prohibit or limit the amount of oil production in the Arctic. And environmental groups are also creating plans to make Arctic shipping safer.

Third, and most importantly, people are trying to stop climate change. And you can, too. If you want to help save polar bears, you should use less electricity and gas, tell government leaders your opinion about the issue of climate change, and get involved with organizations that are working to save polar bears.

So, to summarize, the main threat to polar bears is loss of habitat due to climate change. Related threats are human contact and industrial development. If people don't make changes quickly, polar bears may disappear.

🔊 1.3

1 First, Arctic communities are trying to reduce contact between humans and polar bears.

2 Second, governments have made laws that prohibit or limit the amount of oil production in the Arctic.

3 So, to summarize, the main threat to polar bears is loss of habitat due to climate change.

🔊 1.4

… beautiful, powerful, majestic …

🔊 1.5

… warmer temperatures, floods, droughts, huge storms …

🔊 1.6

1 large, white, strong
2 pandas, sea turtles, chimpanzees, tigers
3 human contact, climate change, industrial development
4 more lights, electric fences, warning plans

🔊 1.7

It's often said that it's cruel to use animals for entertainment. However, I would like to argue against this idea. I know that many animal lovers would disagree with me, but let me explain my point of view.

First of all, keeping animals in zoos helps protect them. For example, many species, such as the giant panda and the snow leopard, are endangered in the wild, so they are safer in zoos. Another point is that zoos have an important educational role. For instance, children can see animals up close. When I was a child, my father took me to the zoo. I learned about exotic animals, and I also learned to care about animals. Modern zoos have improved their conditions. Animals are no longer kept in small cages, and zoos have large areas where animals can feel as if they are in their natural habitat.

To summarize, zoos help protect animals and educate us. In short, modern zoos are comfortable, safe places for wild animals. In conclusion, I believe that we should help zoos by visiting them and donating money.

🔊 1.8

1 First of all, keeping animals in zoos helps protect them.

2 For example, many species, such as the giant panda and the snow leopard, are endangered in the wild.

3 Another point is that zoos have an important educational role.

4 To summarize, zoos help protect animals and educate us.

5 In short, modern zoos are comfortable, safe places for wild animals.

🔊 1.9

Today I'm going to give you some advice for your presentations in class. It's normal to be nervous when you have to speak in front of your class, but there are a few things that you can do to help yourself, and make it easier for your audience to understand you.

First of all, don't read your presentation aloud … and don't memorize it. That's not a good idea. If you do that, you'll speak too fast and nobody will understand you. Instead, use notes to help you remember what to say. Some students write notes on index cards: one card for each point. If you do that, you will speak more naturally, and people will understand you better.

Second, make sure that you can pronounce key words. Pronunciation is very important. Check and practice the pronunciation of important words – especially names or technical terms. Now, your voice. Don't shout, but speak loudly enough so that the people in the back of the room can hear. Emphasize your important points by speaking more clearly and slowly. Pause after each main point. This gives the audience time to process what you are saying. Finally, don't forget how important it is to use signposting language. Phrases like *first of all, second, finally* – I just said that one! – *in conclusion*, and so on ... these phrases are like road signs. They make it much easier for people to follow your presentation.

UNIT 2

▶ Blowing in the Wind: Off-Shore Wind Farms

We humans use a lot of energy, and some traditional energy sources are running out. Where can we find alternative energy sources? These days, one popular source is wind.
In 2013 the largest offshore wind farm opened here in the open sea.
It's called the London Array, and it's located about 12 miles from the southeast coast of England.
How was it possible to build this giant wind farm in the water?
This was the answer.
Discovery is a special ship that can rise completely out of the water on giant "legs". It made a safe building area in the middle of the sea possible.
And it could hold all the parts to build each wind turbine.
These huge pieces of the turbine look like airplane wings. They were designed to get as

much energy as possible, even from light winds. But as you can imagine, they were difficult to assemble, especially in windy weather.
It took a team effort. Everything had to line up perfectly.
Success!
Each one of these wind turbines is almost 400 feet across. That's 120 meters, about as big as the London Eye. And they built 175 of them. Every turbine can provide power for 3,000 homes. So now, because of the London Array wind farm, over half a million homes in England have clean electricity.

🔊 **2.1**

1 Today I want to explain some alternative solutions.
2 As we all know, in order to grow plants we need water and sunlight.
3 I think that desert farms might be a very interesting way to farm in the future.
4 If you add the nutrients to water, you can grow your fruit and vegetables in water.

🔊 **2.2**

Good morning. As you may remember, the last lecture focused on issues of climate change and its causes and effects. Today I want to explain some **alternative solutions** that may help reduce some of the problems related to climate change. The first solution uses solar energy to grow food in the desert. That's right, growing fruit and vegetables in the desert is now possible, and the first desert farms have been built in Australia. First of all, I will explain how farming in the desert works. Then, we will briefly discuss how this type of farming could solve some of the **environmental** problems we are now facing. And finally, we will discuss some possible problems of this **system**.
So, how does it work? As we all know, in order to grow plants we need water and sunlight. While we have a lot of sunlight in the desert, we have very little water. Scientists have decided to combine the modern technology of solar energy with a farming technology called hydroponics. *Hydroponics* means growing plants

in water. In the 1700s, scientists observed that plants don't need to grow in the ground. They need nutrients, to help them grow. Nutrients are like food for the plants. Therefore, if you add the nutrients to water, you can grow your fruit and vegetables in water. NASA scientists have been developing this method of growing food because it could allow us to grow food in any climate – in Antarctica, the Sahara desert, or even on Mars. You might ask how this method of growing plants helps with the problem of global warming. I mean, after all, it uses fresh water, which is a **limited resource** on our planet.

An Australian company, Sundrop Farms, combined hydroponics with solar energy. Traditional farming uses between 60 and 80 percent of our planet's fresh water. However, Sundrop Farms doesn't use fresh water. It uses seawater. Sundrop Farms is only 110 yards – or 100 meters – from the shore. A line of mirrors reflects heat from the sun onto a pipe, a pipe that has oil inside. The hot oil in the pipe heats up seawater, which is kept in special containers. When the seawater reaches 320° F – 160° C – the steam from this process **provides** electricity. Some of the hot water is used to heat the greenhouse during the cold desert nights. The plants grow in the greenhouse – a building with glass walls and a glass ceiling. The rest of the heated water goes to a desalination plant. Desalination is when we remove the salt from seawater to create drinkable water – that is, water that's clean and safe to drink. The desalination plant can produce up to 2,700 gallons – that is 10,000 liters – of fresh water every day. The farmer adds nutrients to the water and then grows fruit and vegetables.

To summarize, the solar energy is used to remove the salt from the seawater, and the fresh water is then used inside the greenhouse, where the plants are growing. As you can imagine, many people around the world are really excited about this technology. So far, Australian farms have grown tomatoes, peppers, and cucumbers in this way. Many supermarkets are interested in buying these vegetables because they are

grown without pesticides or other chemicals. Some people think this is the perfect solution to the world food **crisis**. After all, this way of farming can help us grow food in very difficult conditions. Furthermore, it uses seawater, which is a major advantage.

Finally, the desert farms use solar energy and not fossil fuels, thus their negative effect on the environment is minimal. Now, of course, the future of hydroponics is uncertain. But taking all this into consideration – the quality of food, the use of seawater, and the minimal use of fossil fuels – I think that desert farms might be a very interesting way to farm in the future. Now let's discuss some of the problems …

🔊 2.3

An Australian company, Sundrop Farms, combined hydroponics with solar energy. Traditional farming uses between 60 and 80 percent of our planet's fresh water. However, Sundrop Farms doesn't use fresh water. It uses seawater. Sundrop Farms is only 110 yards – or 100 meters – from the shore. A line of mirrors reflects heat from the sun onto a pipe, a pipe that has oil inside. The hot oil in the pipe heats up seawater, which is kept in special containers. When the seawater reaches 320° F – 160° C – the steam from this process provides electricity. Some of the hot water is used to heat the greenhouse during the cold desert nights. The plants grow in the greenhouse – a building with glass walls and a glass ceiling. The rest of the heated water goes to a desalination plant. Desalination is when we remove the salt from seawater to create drinkable water – that is, water that's clean and safe to drink. The desalination plant can produce up to 2,700 gallons – that is 10,000 liters – of fresh water every day. The farmer adds nutrients to the water and then grows fruit and vegetables.

To summarize, the solar energy is used to remove the salt from the seawater, and the fresh water is then used inside the greenhouse, where the plants are growing. As you can imagine, many people around the world are really excited about this technology. So far, Australian farms

nuclear Power

have grown tomatoes, peppers, and cucumbers in this way. Many supermarkets are interested in buying these vegetables because they are grown without pesticides or other chemicals. Some people think this is the perfect solution to the world food crisis. After all, this way of farming can help us grow food in very difficult conditions. Furthermore, it uses seawater, which is a major advantage.

Finally, the desert farms use solar energy and not fossil fuels, thus their negative effect on the environment is minimal. Now, of course, the future of hydroponics is uncertain. But taking all this into consideration – the quality of food, the use of seawater, and the minimal use of fossil fuels – I think that desert farms might be a very interesting way to farm in the future. Now let's discuss some of the problems …

🔊 2.4

1 Today I want to explain some alternative solutions that may help reduce some of the problems related to climate change.

2 NASA scientists have been developing this method of growing food because it could allow us to grow food in any climate.

3 I think that desert farms might be a very interesting way to farm in the future.

🔊 2.5

Host: Welcome to today's debate on the advantages and disadvantages of nuclear energy. Some people think that nuclear power is an environmentally friendly source of energy because it creates less pollution than traditional power plants. However, the **opponents** of nuclear energy believe that it has more dangers than **benefits**. Debating this issue today are Emma Martinez and Jack Sullivan. Thank you for joining us today to share your opinions about this important issue.

Emma: Thank you. I want to argue that there are many problems with nuclear power. It may be true that there are very few accidents caused by nuclear plants, but if there is an accident, then it will be huge, and it will have **long-term** effects on the environment. For example, after

the Fukushima nuclear **disaster** in Japan, the government had to tell people to leave their homes because of the possibility of radiation. The radioactive material spread to water and food, such as tea, milk, beef, and fish. For months after the accident, the Fukushima plant was dangerous. People will not be able to live in the nearby area for the next 20 years. This is the big **risk** of building a nuclear power plant. Now I'm not antigovernment, but in my opinion, it's irresponsible for governments to allow nuclear power plants to be built near cities. They're just too dangerous.

Jack: I have to disagree. I think we should look at the bigger picture. Some people are worried that nuclear power is a big risk. Despite that, there are hundreds of nuclear power plants all over the world, and there have only been three major nuclear accidents in the last 30 years. In fact, research shows that many more people die while working with coal, natural gas, and hydropower – that is, electricity powered by water. Furthermore, nuclear power is the most environmentally friendly and the most sustainable source of energy. In other words, it doesn't damage the environment, and there will always be enough of it. A nuclear power plant does not **pollute** the air, it is relatively cheap, and it can provide a huge amount of electricity to our cities. And of course, our cities are growing—

Emma: I'm sorry, can I interrupt? Some people say that nuclear energy doesn't pollute the air, but that's not completely true. It takes many years to build a nuclear power plant. During this time, hundreds of machines work day and night and pollute the air in the area. I don't think it's necessary to build nuclear power plants when we have safer and more environmentally friendly energy sources, such as solar and wind energy. They are cheaper and they are unlimited sources of energy. Furthermore, they are more **affordable** for most countries, when compared with nuclear power. Building a nuclear power plant is not a solution for poor or developing countries.

Jack: I'm not sure about that. I think that building nuclear power plants is the perfect solution for many poorer countries. Yes, it might be expensive to build the plant, but once the nuclear plant is there, the cost of the production of energy is very low. What's more, the country can sell the electricity to its neighbors and improve its economy. It's a long-term solution. Moreover, it makes a country less dependent on oil and gas. At the moment, whenever oil or gas prices go up, it's the poor countries and poor people who suffer. Some people think that solar and wind energy are greener than nuclear energy. However, I don't think that's accurate. Wind turbines are not exactly friendly for birds, not to mention that solar panels and wind turbines take up a lot of space. They are also very expensive and do not last as long as a nuclear power plant. In short, wind and solar energy can't solve the problem of climate change, and they aren't a good solution for poor countries.

Host: Thank you both very much. Let's take some questions from the audience ...

🔊 2.6

Interviewer: Today we're speaking to Dr. Eileen Ferraro. She's going to talk about active learning: what it is and why it's important for college students. Welcome to the show.

Dr. Ferraro: Thank you.

Interviewer: First, what is active learning?

Dr. Ferraro: Well, most students know that in college, you have to read a lot of books and listen to a lot of lectures. But active learning involves more than that. It means interacting with the material ... thinking about it, talking about it, using it. If students don't interact with the material, they don't really learn it.

Interviewer: Can you give us an example of what you mean?

Dr. Ferraro: Well, for example, when you read, maybe you underline important points in your textbook. But to really learn it, you should do more than that. For example, you could summarize the chapter in your own words.

Interviewer: I see.

Dr. Ferraro: Some students like to transfer material into a different format. I had a student once who made presentations of the information in every chapter, with visuals.

Interviewer: That's a great idea!

Dr. Ferraro: Yes. It helped him to remember it. Then, he would explain the material to his study group. Teaching other people is a really good way to learn.

Interviewer: I see. So that's why teachers ask students to give presentations.

Dr. Ferraro: Yes. But it's not just about remembering information. In college we also expect students to evaluate what they read. This means asking questions. Most teachers love questions because it means that the students are thinking about the material, and trying to connect it to their own experience.

Interviewer: I suppose project work is another example of active learning.

Dr. Ferraro: Exactly. Yes.

Interviewer: But it's much more difficult, in some ways.

Dr. Ferraro: Yes! And some students are not used to this way of learning. But we know that this is how students learn the most.

UNIT 3

▶ **The Air Travel Revolution**
In the past 50 years we've done the impossible — we've made the world smaller. Today we can travel from continent to continent in no time. Paris and London are closer than ever before. North America and Europe are almost neighbors. And South America and Asia are less than a day away from each other.

Trips that used to happen once in a lifetime now happen weekly for many business people.

How have we done this? By taking to the air.

Airplanes have clearly revolutionized transportation.

Military planes travel faster than the speed of sound.

Commercial planes like the Airbus A380 and the Boeing 747 are much bigger than houses. More people travel by air than ever in history.

The airspace over London, for example, is among the busiest and most crowded in the world.

Every day 3,500 flights take place overhead. And that's just one city.

In 2016, about 3.7 billion people traveled by plane. And that number will likely continue to grow.

The sky has become a place for us to work, rest, and play.

And right now, around the world, over a million people are traveling in the air above us.

◀)) 3.1

1 There has been an increase in motorcycle accidents over the past five years.

2 Airlines are always looking for new ways to increase the safety of their planes.

◀)) 3.2

1 There's a detailed record of each plane crash.

2 A machine called a "black box" records everything that the pilot and copilot say during a flight.

3 Some cities don't permit biking on the sidewalk.

4 I'm sorry, but you need an employee parking permit to park in this garage.

5 The company presents an award for road safety to the safest city.

6 He received a new car as a birthday present.

◀)) 3.3

Host: Have you ever been afraid of flying? Do you feel **scared** when you sit on a plane? Are you stressed when there's turbulence? If so, you may have aerophobia. The word *aerophobia* comes from the Greek, and it **consists of** two parts: *aero*, which means "flight" or "air," and *phobia*, which means "fear." People with aerophobia experience **extreme** fear or panic when they sit on a plane. In today's program, we'll discuss some steps that you can take to reduce this fear. With me today is Mark Knowling. Mark used to be a flight attendant who was afraid of flying. He has written a book about his experience and often gives presentations to help other people deal with their phobias. Can you tell us more about your experience, Mark?

Mark: Yes, sure. So I took a flight attendant's course right after college. My goal was to see the world, and I thought it would be a good job for me. I learned a lot more than I expected from the course. During the training, we studied a lot about air **safety**, but there were also lectures about plane **crashes**. The instructors would tell us horrible stories of serious problems – broken engines, birds hitting the aircraft, hijackings, and even stories of planes crashing in the middle of the desert or in the ocean.

Host: That's terrible!

Mark: No, I don't think so. They were trying to make us take the job seriously. They would also discuss the research done by air crash investigators to help us understand the reasons behind air crashes. There's a detailed record of each crash, which investigators check carefully.

Host: But for you, I suppose this training had the opposite effect. How did it influence you? Did it make you afraid of flying?

Mark: Uh-huh, the course had a strong impact on me. I actually became very scared of being on a plane. When I told my colleagues about it, they just laughed. They couldn't believe that I had completed the flight attendant training and now I was afraid to get on a plane. What was I supposed to do? I decided to research it online, and I read stories about people who managed to control their fear of flying.

Host: Can it be cured?

Mark: Actually, like any phobia, there's not always a **cure** for it, but you can decrease its effects on your life. You need to have the right attitude. You can achieve anything if you concentrate and stay positive. The advice I got was very useful, but it was a challenge, and it took me a long time to get over my fear.

🔊 **3.4**

Host: Can you share some advice with our listeners?

Mark: Of course. Well, the first method to decrease your fear is to learn more about how planes work. For example, many people believe that without the engines, the plane will simply fall down from the sky, but that isn't true. The plane will stay up because its wings push against the air. A plane can fly without the engines, and a well-trained pilot will be able to control it without power. All pilots learn how to fly without the engines.

Host: What about turbulence? Whenever I fly, I get very scared during turbulence.

Mark: Well, turbulence can be dangerous, of course. However, most turbulence is completely normal and won't cause any trouble, so you shouldn't be afraid of it. The only situation where it can cause problems is when the aircraft is already damaged or during a storm. But, as you know, airlines study the weather and won't carry passengers if they think the weather conditions aren't safe for flying.

Host: Is there any other advice that you can give?

Mark: Understanding where the emergency exits are may help you relax. Not knowing where an exit is and feeling that you're in a closed space can make you afraid. Finally, to decrease the fear of flying, you should **avoid** watching movies about plane crashes or other accidents. Some researchers say that aerophobia is caused by people watching too many disaster movies. I think we often forget that, compared to the many forms of transportation that we use every day, air transportation is actually very safe.

Host: In what way?

Mark: Well, there's research that **compares** the number of accidents per number of miles traveled on each form of transportation. We can see that by far the safest form of travel is air transportation, and the most dangerous is using a motorcycle. In recent years, there has been a significant decrease in the number of plane crashes. In contrast, cars are considerably more dangerous.

Host: Really? I didn't know that. Thank you for your advice, Mark. You can let us know what you think about air safety and share your stories by going to our website at www ...

🔊 **3.5**

1 The course was a lot more challenging than I expected.

2 We can see that by far the most affordable form of transportation is walking.

3 The risks of driving a car are considerably more significant than those of flying.

4 For me, flying is much more comfortable than traveling by train.

5 Taking a train is definitely more relaxing than driving.

🔊 **3.6**

Hello, everyone. Thank you for being here today. Welcome to the first meeting of Wheels to Work. As you know, the goal of this group is to make our city more bike-friendly. Specifically, we'd like to make it easier for people to ride their bikes to work. Biking to work is good for the environment, and it provides great exercise. And personally, I think it's a lot of fun!

I'm hoping that we can work together to **solve** the problems that can make it difficult for city residents to bike to work. Today I'm going to talk about a few of those problems and share some ideas for solving them.

So, the biggest issue is safety. A lot of people would love to ride their bikes to work, but they're scared – they feel that it's just too dangerous. This is because there's a lot of traffic during rush hour, when most people drive to or from work, and there's very little space for bikers. Many of the bike lanes we have are too narrow, and some of the busiest streets don't even have bike lanes. What's more, many drivers don't have **respect** for bikers. Cars sometimes even drive in the bike lanes to **pass** other cars. Of course, if a car hits a bike, it's going to **injure** or even kill the biker.

A second issue is storage. Many people don't have a safe place to put their bikes while they're at work. They worry that if they leave their bike outside, it'll get stolen. Also, it'll get wet when it rains and might get damaged over time.

A third problem is that, for some people, riding a bike to work isn't **convenient**. Maybe they live far from their job, or maybe they sometimes work late and don't want to bike home in the dark. And a lot of people don't like to bike in the rain. What if you ride your bike to work, and then later it starts raining? From my own experience, I can tell you that it's pretty terrible to ride home during a storm.

So, those are three of the biggest issues: safety, storage, and convenience.

🔊 3.7

Now I'd like to share some possible solutions. First, to improve safety, I'd suggest that police officers give big **fines** to drivers who **break the law** by driving in a bike lane.

Also, I'd like to see wider bike lanes to allow more bicycles to pass at the same time. We should also add bike lanes to busy streets that don't have them yet. These proposals would **prevent** cars from hitting bikers and would save lives.

As for the issue of storage, I think that city parking garages ought to create special parking sections for bikes. This would keep bikes safe and dry while people are working.

Finally, convenience. In my opinion, we should make it easier to bring bikes on public transportation. For example, we could put bike racks on the outside of buses. That way, people wouldn't have to ride their bikes at night or in bad weather. And people who live far from work could bike part of the way to work and take public transportation the rest of the way. As a result, more people could bike to work.

Well, thank you again for listening to my ideas. I hope this is the beginning of a conversation about how we can make this a great city for bikers!

🔊 3.8

A: I'm really surprised by these statistics. I didn't know that eating while driving is dangerous. I don't think the government should do anything about it. Personally, I eat fast food in my car a few times a week, and I've never had an accident. And I'm not convinced that driving while eating is a big problem. Have you ever eaten while driving?

B: No, I haven't. We should take this really seriously. I think it would be better if they closed drive-through restaurants. This is because they only encourage drivers to buy food and eat it while they drive. How can you focus on the road if you're holding a big burger in your hand? It seems dangerous to me. What do you think?

C: I completely agree. I think it would be much better if drivers weren't allowed to eat or drink while they drive. From my own experience, I can tell you that it can be very dangerous. Last week, I bought some coffee and something to eat on the way to work. As I was driving, I had to brake suddenly and I spilled hot coffee over my legs. I almost lost control of the car. I think the police should give heavy fines if they see someone doing it.

D: OK, I understand, but it might be very difficult for the police to see drivers eating, especially if they're driving fast. The best thing would be to have more cameras on the roads to record what drivers are doing. The reason for this is the police can check the videos to see who's eating, who's texting, and so on. Then, I'd suggest that the police give the drivers points on their license. If the driver has a lot of points, the police should take their car away for a few months.

🔊 3.9

Today we're looking at your goals for the future. Of course, it's important for students to have goals, and I'm sure most of you do. But sometimes it's difficult to turn your goals into a reality! I'm going to introduce the SMART criteria as a way to help you achieve those goals. SMART goals are specific, measurable, achievable, relevant, and time-bound. I'll explain these one by one.

First, your goal should be specific. Many students have goals like, "I want to get a good job," but that's not really specific enough. For a goal to be effective, you need to identify what you want in detail. What is a "good job"?

Second, you need to make sure that your goal is measurable. How will you measure your progress? Decide how many hours you'll spend in the gym each week, or how much weight you would like to lose.

Third, your goal needs to be achievable. A goal like "I'm going to get an A in all of my classes" may not be achievable if your average grade is a C. One like "I'm going to get at least a B+ in two classes" might be more realistic. Also, ask yourself how. "How am I going to do this? What steps do I need to take?" For example, you might need to study more regularly, or get a tutor.

The fourth letter, R, stands for *relevant*. A relevant goal is one that is linked to your long-term objectives. Ask yourself, "How important is this in the long term?"

Finally, your goal needs to be time-bound. This means that you should decide on a schedule for achieving your goal. What will you do this week? Next week? Before the end of the semester?

So SMART goals are goals that are specific, measurable, achievable, relevant, and time-bound. Any questions? No?

Right. Next, we'll look at the steps … [fade]

UNIT 4

▶ The Chilean Cueca Brava

In Chile, the *cueca brava*, or Chilean *cueca*, is a national dance. The rhythm and the steps express the soul of the nation. It is a variety of the cueca style of music and dance which is well known in Argentina, Chile, and Bolivia.

The cueca is especially popular in the countryside, but on Chile's National Day,

September 18th, people everywhere can be seen dancing the cueca brava.

The singer here is Daniel Muñoz, who is a TV and movie actor, as well as a singer, from Chile. He's a strong supporter of the cueca brava's status as the people's dance.

In central Chile, the guitar, accordion, and percussion instruments like the tambourine are among the most common instruments seen at the dance.

Having a handkerchief to wave is essential at a cueca brava. Traditionally, a man and a woman face each other, hold their handkerchief in the air, and then begin to dance. If a real handkerchief is not available, a paper napkin can be used instead. The dance takes the form of a complex courtship between a rooster and his lady bird.

These men are wearing the black hats of *huasos* – skilled horsemen from the countryside.

The dance is enjoyed by both younger and older generations, and there is no doubt that it will continue to be a symbol of the nation for many years to come.

🔊 4.1

This Sunday on *Book of the Week*, we interview Kevin Lee, a well-known anthropologist and the author of *Changing Traditions in the Modern World.* In this program, we will discuss his love for cultural anthropology and whether traditions are adapting to the modern world or dying out. Join us at 1 p.m.

🔊 4.2

Host: Welcome to this week's book review. In the studio with me is Dr. Kevin Lee, professor of anthropology and the author of the best-selling book *Changing Traditions in the Modern World*. First of all, could you tell us what anthropologists study and what your own area of interest is?

Dr. Lee: That's a good question! Anthropology, in a general sense, is the study of humanity. I know that's not very exact. That's why we have many types of anthropology, like linguistic anthropology and **social** anthropology. My specialty is cultural anthropology. I study different cultures around the world and how social and **political** changes affect these cultures.

Host: And when did you first become interested in anthropology?

Dr. Lee: I grew up in a **multicultural** home. My mother is American and my father is Korean. They were both English teachers, so we traveled a lot. As a child, I lived in Japan, Thailand, and Egypt. That's why I decided to study anthropology. Growing up in different cultures helps you realize that customs and traditions are often local. Things that are acceptable in one culture can be completely unacceptable in another. However, despite some differences between cultures, I have noticed that there are often more similarities than differences between people.

Host: And do traditions change?

Dr. Lee: Absolutely, customs and traditions change all the time. Some traditions **die out** because our way of life changes, but most traditions adapt.

Host: As I understand it, that's one of the main points of your latest book.

Dr. Lee: Yes. My book is about the effect of modern technology on traditions around the world. It's well known that things such as electricity, the telephone, and television have changed our lives significantly. The introduction of these inventions into our lives has changed many of our customs. For example, in the past, families spent time playing board games or listening to the radio in the evening. These activities would deepen family relationships. Now, due to developments in technology, people spend more time **interacting** with other people over the Internet.

Host: Is that a bad thing?

Dr. Lee: I don't think so. There are people who complain about the changes that technology has brought to our lives. Personally, I think these changes are fine. We still spend time interacting with other people, but it's not always face-to-face.

Host: In your book, you discuss how technology has changed the way we celebrate important holidays.

Dr. Lee: That's right. A simple example is sending cards or messages. In the past, people sent each other cards to celebrate important events like birthdays and **anniversaries**. But now, more people send messages through social networking sites or by email. Another example of changing customs is holiday food. A few **generations** ago, people spent a lot of time and effort preparing special meals for **celebrations**. It was usually the women who did this. Some dishes could take up to a week to prepare. But now we don't have to work so hard. This is because we have modern kitchens and supermarket food. We don't have to spend endless hours making our own butter or bread anymore. Everything is quicker and easier now.

Host: Hmm ... I remember my grandmother working for days to make food. She had a huge cookbook that she got from her grandmother. Everything had to be exactly as it was when she was a little girl.

Dr. Lee: That's a good example of a tradition that has been replaced by technology. You can find any recipe you want on the Internet. This means that many people don't need cookbooks anymore. Another thing is that many families now go out instead of cooking at home. In India, for example, families hire catering companies to provide food for weddings or special occasions. In the United States, on Thanksgiving, which is one of the biggest celebrations, many families go to restaurants because they don't want to spend their holiday working in the kitchen.

Host: So people do continue their tradition of eating a special meal – they just do it in a different way.

Dr. Lee: Yes. Traditions don't always die out – but customs and traditions do change and adapt to the modern world.

🔊 4.3

1 Anthropology, in a general sense, is the study of humanity. I know that's not very exact. That's why we have many types of anthropology, like linguistic anthropology and social anthropology.

2 Some traditions die out because our way of life changes.

3 Now, due to developments in technology, people spend more time interacting with other people over the Internet.

4 But now we don't have to work so hard. This is because we have modern kitchens and supermarket food.

5 In the United States, on Thanksgiving, which is one of the biggest celebrations, many families go to restaurants because they don't want to spend their holiday working in the kitchen.

🔊 4.4

I study different cultures around the world and how social and political changes affect these cultures.

🔊 4.5

1 My book is about the effect of modern technology on traditions around the world.

2 People spent a lot of time and effort preparing special meals.

3 Growing up in different cultures helps you realize that customs and traditions are often local.

4 We still spend time interacting with other people, but it's not always face-to-face.

5 In the past, people sent each other cards to celebrate important events like birthdays and anniversaries.

6 Traditions don't always die out – but customs and traditions do change and adapt to the modern world.

🔊 4.6

Gabriela: So, our assignment is to discuss customs that have been changing recently – you know, how modern lifestyles have changed people's **behavior**. Any ideas?

Yildiz: Hmm ... Let me think. Well, holidays are one kind of custom. Can you think of any holidays that have changed?

David: Oh, don't talk about holidays! It reminds me that Mother's Day is in two days, and I haven't gotten a gift for my mom yet.

Gabriela: Yeah, I haven't either. Who has time for shopping when we have so much work to do?

David: I agree. I get tired of shopping for gifts. I actually don't know why we have to get gifts for every little holiday. Wouldn't our mothers be just as happy if we just spent time with them – you know, made it a special **event**, like taking them out to lunch at a nice restaurant? How did this whole gift giving for every holiday tradition get started, anyway? It seems silly to me.

Gabriela: That's it! There's our topic! How holidays have become too **commercial**.

🔊 4.7

Yildiz: Hold on, too commercial? I disagree. I like giving gifts. I think that it shows that you were thinking of someone.

David: Because you went out and got someone some chocolate or jewelry or a scarf or something at the last minute? Everyone knows that people usually buy gifts because it's an **obligation**, not because they really want to.

Yildiz: Well, you have to spend time thinking about the gift, and get something **thoughtful**, you know, **personal**. Like maybe the new book by their favorite author.

Gabriela: I see your point. But I'm not convinced because then you have to spend money ... money that could be spent on more important things. Also, all that time you spent shopping you could have instead spent with the person you're shopping for.

David: I couldn't agree more. And it's not just holidays that are a problem – personally, I think we give too many gifts for other special **occasions**, too. Like when my sister **graduated** from high school last year, she got lots of gifts. And money, too. The focus was all on opening gifts. I've heard that when people receive more than a few gifts, they usually can't even remember who gave them which gift. Instead, why not write letters of advice for the future? That would be more special.

Gabriela: That's a great idea!

Yildiz: Sorry, I don't agree. I doubt that graduates would be happy if we changed that custom! I think that graduation gifts are practical. Don't young people need some gifts and money for starting their new life? And they can always look at the gift and think of the person who gave it to them. I think it's a nice custom.

Gabriela: I'm still really not convinced. I mean ...

🔊 4.8

Gabriela: So, our assignment is to discuss customs that have been changing recently – you know, how modern lifestyles have changed people's behavior. Any ideas?

Yildiz: Hmm ... Let me think. Well, holidays are one kind of custom. Can you think of any holidays that have changed?

David: Oh, don't talk about holidays! It reminds me that Mother's Day is in two days, and I haven't gotten a gift for my mom yet.

Gabriela: Yeah, I haven't either. Who has time for shopping when we have so much work to do?

David: I agree. I get tired of shopping for gifts. I actually don't know why we have to get gifts for every little holiday. Wouldn't our mothers be just as happy if we just spent time with them – you know, made it a special event, like taking them out to lunch at a nice restaurant? How did this whole gift giving for every holiday tradition get started, anyway? It seems silly to me.

Gabriela: That's it! There's our topic! How holidays have become too commercial.

Yildiz: Hold on, too commercial? I disagree. I like giving gifts. I think that it shows that you were thinking of someone.

David: Because you went out and got someone some chocolate or jewelry or a scarf or something at the last minute? Everyone knows that people usually buy gifts because it's an obligation, not because they really want to.

Yildiz: Well, you have to spend time thinking about the gift, and get something thoughtful, you know, personal. Like maybe the new book by their favorite author.

Gabriela: I see your point. But I'm not convinced because then you have to spend money ... money that could be spent on more important things. Also, all that time you spent shopping you could have instead spent with the person you're shopping for.

David: I couldn't agree more. And it's not just holidays that are a problem – personally, I think we give too many gifts for other special occasions, too. Like when my sister graduated from high school last year, she got lots of gifts. And money, too. The focus was all on opening gifts. I've heard that when people receive more than a few gifts, they usually can't even remember who gave them which gift. Instead, why not write letters of advice for the future? That would be more special.

Gabriela: That's a great idea!

Yildiz: Sorry, I don't agree. I doubt that graduates would be happy if we changed that custom! I think that graduation gifts are practical. Don't young people need some gifts and money for starting their new life? And they can always look at the gift and think of the person who gave it to them. I think it's a nice custom.

Gabriela: I'm still really not convinced. I mean ...

🔊 4.9

1 I couldn't agree more.

2 How did this whole gift giving for every holiday tradition get started, anyway? It seems silly to me.

3 I agree. I get tired of shopping for gifts.

4 I disagree. I like giving gifts.

5 But I'm not convinced because then you have to spend money ... money that could be spent on more important things.

6 Instead, why not write letters of advice for the future? That would be more special.

7 Sorry, I don't agree. I doubt that graduates would be happy if we changed that custom!

🔊 **4.10**

I completely agree that holidays have become too commercial.

I absolutely disagree that we should stop giving gifts on Mother's Day.

I really think that we should give fewer gifts.

🔊 **4.11**

Alisha: My first semester at the university was very difficult. I couldn't understand anything … and the worst thing was I couldn't speak. So, often I knew the answer, but I couldn't say it fast enough. I felt so stupid. I was a good student at home and I could always answer the teacher's questions. I was very frustrated, and I wanted to go home. But my English classes were very helpful. I learned some strategies for taking notes and studying, and bit by bit I began to understand more. It just got better after that.

John: My problem was the food. I really didn't like anything. It was all too sweet and there was cheese on everything. I hate cheese. So for the first couple of weeks I didn't eat very much … and then I got sick. It was awful! But then some friends showed me a cheap restaurant near the campus where I could get Chinese food. I was so happy when I found food I could eat! I've gotten more used to American food now, but I still go there a lot.

Minh: I was the only international student in my dorm and everybody else was American. They were always very friendly, but I found it hard to understand if they were really friends. They'd say "Let's get together sometime!" but then they'd never call. I couldn't understand why they did that. Later I realized they weren't really inviting me. It's just the culture. They were just being polite.

UNIT 5

▶ Yoga in California Schools

Katherine Priore: Warrior clap, one, two, three. One, two three. One, two, three.

Reporter: Warriors alike, ready for their next challenge.

Katherine Priore: And go for it. Warrior three.

Reporter: Whether it's reading, math, or simply finding the strength to focus in class.

Katherine Priore: Sometimes it takes a lot of courage to just be a little bit more still and not busy.

Reporter: How many of you think that yoga has made a difference in your life? Everybody.

Boy: I'm open, like, my mind's comfortable.

Girl 1: I forget about like the bad things that are happening.

Girl 2: I feel happy and like calm.

Katherine Priore: Let it go.

Reporter: It was a difference Katherine Priore noticed more than a decade ago.

Katherine Priore: That also takes some courage opening up that hard area. That can be scary.

Reporter: When she first turned to yoga as a stressed-out school teacher.

Katherine Priore: I think a real benefit is learning a process for internal listening.

Reporter: If it worked for her, why not the overworked kids in her classroom?

Katherine Priore: Take a deep breath into that.

Reporter: In 2008, Priore founded Headstand, a nonprofit dedicated to bringing yoga into schools.

Katherine Priore: *Yoga* is simply a word to define the connection between your mind, your emotion, and your physical well-being.

Male teacher: Page three is about the first passage.

Katherine Priore: Ninety-eight percent of our students say that after yoga class they're more ready to learn.

Reporter: The 400 students at San Lorenzo, California's KIPP Summit Academy need that focus.

Katherine Priore: Hands to your heart.

Reporter: Since bringing Headstand to KIPP, suspensions are down 60%, while state test scores are up. But the benefits stretch far beyond the school day.

Girl 3: A lot of time I get mad like at my brother or my sister and then just go to my room and like do yoga for a while. And then I go back out.

Reporter: What are some of the things that you think about or that you look inside yourself for?

Girl 4: I start thinking if I'm wrong or like the reason why I'm fighting, why am I fighting? If I'm wrong, what should I say? Should I apologize?

Reporter: Simple, yet poignant lessons with a daily impact. And for Katherine Priore, proof of the lasting power of yoga.

🔊 5.1

Host: Today we're talking about the key to a long and happy life. Recent studies of people who live to be 100 years old have shown that a healthy diet and exercise may not be enough. In fact, many of the people who celebrate their hundredth birthday have not eaten a healthy diet and have never exercised regularly. This has led many people to believe that our lifestyles are not important. What's most important is that we have good genes. It seems that if you have the right genes, then you'll live for a long time, whatever you do.

🔊 5.2

Host: So, new research shows that having a healthy lifestyle is not the most important thing if you want to live a long life. We asked four people on the street for their reactions to this news.

A: I think it's great news! Most people think that if they eat healthy food and exercise a lot, they'll live forever. These people never drink coffee or sugary drinks. They spend hours **working out** in the gym or doing yoga. And none of this matters if you have the wrong genes. I think that the key to a healthy life is to enjoy yourself. If you focus all your energy on what to do and what not to do, you'll be unhappy eventually. There's no question that happy people live longer. I'd much rather go out and have a pizza with friends than spend time in the gym.

B: This research **proves** what I've known for a long time. It's ridiculous to get too worried about healthy eating and exercise. My grandfather lived until he was 95, even though he never exercised. He ate lots of sugar and never ate vegetables. He was brought up in a different world. He had different **habits**. He certainly never went to a gym. Yes, I'm sure that genes are more important than our lifestyle. Of course, I'm not going to give up exercising or start eating fast food every day. The research shows I should stay in shape because it makes me feel better – but I won't allow fitness to take over my whole life.

C: Well, first of all, I prefer to exercise and eat well. What's wrong with being healthy? I also think that you won't know whether or not you have the right genes until you get sick. So why take the risk and be **unhealthy**? Also, don't forget that you might get the flu or a cold much more easily when you don't eat healthy food or exercise. I'd say that it's always better to have a healthy lifestyle. There's no doubt that bad health habits increase the chances of getting a serious **illness**.

D: Oh, that's great. So now we should all eat fast food and stop exercising? I mean I look around and I see **overweight** children everywhere. No matter how good their genes are, I'm sure that these children won't be able to enjoy a long and healthy life unless they give up chips, chocolate bars, sugary drinks ... Well, it's great that some people can live to be 100 and do whatever they want in their lives, but I prefer to be careful and take care of myself because I don't know if I have good genes!

🔊 5.3

I'm really surprised about that.
I'm really surprised about that!

🔊 5.4

1 I think it's great news!
2 There's no question that happy people live longer.
3 It's ridiculous to get too worried about healthy eating and exercise!
4 Oh, that's great. So now we should all eat fast food and stop exercising?

5 Well, it's great that some people can live to be 100 and do whatever they want in their lives, but ...

🔊 5.5

Presenter 1: Do you feel tired? Are you under a lot of **stress**? Do you have problems concentrating on your work? If so, it's time to take up meditation – the practice of thinking calm thoughts in order to **relax**. As we all know, meditation can improve your health and your emotional well-being. It also has **mental** benefits – it has been shown to improve **concentration**. This ancient practice is known to increase your energy and lead to a happier life. Whether you're looking for a stress-free life, physical well-being, or self-discovery, Sanjee Meditation has it all. Sign up now for a free introductory class, starting on January 15th.

Presenter 2: Would you like to improve your social life, your intellectual **performance**, your physical fitness, and your team-building skills? Scientific research has proven that team sports offer all of these benefits. Join us and take advantage of the many benefits of team sports. We're a group of energetic adults of all ages who get together on Sunday afternoons to play soccer, and we're always looking for new players to join in the fun. Whether you've been playing soccer for years or want to take up a new sport, you're welcome to **participate**. Everyone can play – you don't even need to try out! If you're interested in learning more about our group, check out our website at www.soccersundays.cup.com. Sign up today, and you can be part of a team as early as this weekend! Hope to see you on the field soon!

Presenter 3: Hi, my name's Angie Stratton, and I'm the director of CultureCycle. CultureCycle is a new concept in travel: educational fitness touring! We offer courses all over the world that combine learning with exercise and travel. Each course has an educational theme, such as Brazilian cooking or the history of Turkey. As a small group, we bike from place to place, stopping for several days in each location to rest, relax, and do some hands-on learning. Not

only does this trip provide terrific exercise and a fascinating cultural experience, it's the best way to learn. There's no question that physical activity improves our memory and thinking skills – so after a few days of biking, your brain will be ready to learn. So be kind to your body and your mind, and come with us on an amazing adventure you'll never forget!

Presenter 4: Are you interested in alternative **treatments**? Have you ever wanted to explore the secrets of traditional Chinese medicine? This spring, join our six-month course in acupuncture – a treatment for pain or illness that involves putting needles under your skin at special points on the body. The course covers the theory of acupuncture and practical skills in using needles. Acupuncture is known to **reduce** pain, but it's also a great alternative for people who want to lose weight in an easy way. Learn more about the course and visit us on our open house days on the first Saturday of every month.

🔊 5.6

Interviewer: Welcome to the program. This morning we're going to be talking about college students and health. And here to talk to us about this issue is Doctor Mirna Pham, author of the book *Healthy Body, Healthy Mind*. Welcome to the program.

Dr. Pham: Thank you.

Interviewer: First, what kind of health issues do college students have?

Dr. Pham: Well, there's no question that the biggest problem is stress. Students have so much going on: classes, homework, part-time jobs, extracurricular activities ... it's a lot. And many young people haven't learned how to handle that kind of pressure. So they tend to eat badly, stay up all night to finish assignments, and so on.

Interviewer: And that just makes things worse.

Dr. Pham: Yes. They get tired, and then they get more stressed out.

Interviewer: So what do you recommend?

Dr. Pham: Make time for regular exercise.

Interviewer: Really? But they're already so busy!

Dr. Pham: Yes, but all the research shows that exercise is a great way to beat stress ... and it actually helps you study better.

Interviewer: Why is that?

Dr. Pham: Exercise increases blood flow to the brain, so it works better. If you exercise regularly, you can focus better, and remember more.

Interviewer: So working out can make you a better student?

Dr. Pham: Absolutely. Better than staying up all night!

Interviewer: That makes sense.

Dr. Pham: People who exercise sleep better, too. And getting enough sleep is so important. Most people need between 7 and 9 hours a night. Unfortunately, many college students don't get that much.

Interviewer: No.

Dr. Pham: They sleep better ... and they also eat better.

Interviewer: Yes ... So exercise has a positive effect in other ways.

Dr. Pham: The thing is, students in college are establishing a pattern for the future. If they don't start good habits now, it'll be difficult for them to change later. College really is the time to start taking care of your health for the rest of your life.

UNIT 6

▶ A Helping Hand

Anna Werner (reporter): Ask first grader Holden Mora how his new hand works, and he'll be happy to demonstrate.

Holden Mora: So when I bend my hand in like this, it closes. When I bend it this, it opens.

Anna Werner: At seven years old, he's become an expert on the workings of this novel device made out of plastic for roughly $20.

Holden Mora: It's an amazing $20.

Anna Werner: It's an amazing $20.

Holden Mora: And normally, the materials cost a lot. About, like, $1,000.

Anna Werner: He's right. Children like Holden, born without hands or fingers, in his case the fingers on his left hand, often require custom prosthetic replacements costing thousands of dollars. But this inexpensive device was created by a college student using a 3D printer.

Jeff Powell: It builds it layer by layer.

Anna Werner: Senior Jeff Powell studies biomedical engineering at the University of North Carolina at Chapel Hill. He took on the project after learning about Holden from one of his professors.

Jeff Powell: OK, try that now.

Anna Werner: He used instructions posted on the Internet, called the Cyborg Beast, then customized it. The 3D printer builds the parts in under 24 hours. And at the end, what you wind up with, is this.

Jeff Powell: Yes.

Anna Werner: Right.

Jeff Powell: Yes. So the way this works is it straps onto Holden's hand and onto the end of his forearm. When he moves his wrist in, the fingers close. When he moves his wrist out, the fingers open.

Anna Werner: And, do that again. Do they have grip strengths? So, oh, they actually do have grip strength.

Jeff Powell: Yes.

Anna Werner: His goal: for Holden to be able to do things the rest of us take for granted.

Jeff Powell: To be able to eat dinner while holding, you know, a knife and a fork at the same time. To be able to grab onto his scooter or his bike with two hands. Maybe even, you know, swing a baseball bat if we get it that strong enough. I don't want him to be limited by the condition that he was born with.

Anna Werner: So this isn't just about a hand for him, is it?

Jeff Powell: No, no. It's about enabling him to do anything that he wants to do.

Anna Werner: And the payoff for this amateur designer? When he picked up a cup, you were able to say to yourself, "Hey, this worked."

Jeff Powell: Yes, yes.

Anna Werner: That had to be a great moment.

Jeff Powell: Yes. It was nice to see it all pay off.

Anna Werner: Powell has now started a crowdfunding campaign to raise money so other kids can get the device too.

Holden Mora: Well, I'm actually really happy because I think it's true that once I get the best hand, they'll make more like it for those kids. And then they'll have the best kind of hand too.

Anna Werner: Eleven more children are already waiting for their new hands. For CBS *This Morning*, Anna Werner, Chapel Hill, North Carolina.

🔊 6.1

Welcome to the Museum of Science! The exhibition that we're about to see is called ***Discovering*** Medieval Science. As some of you may know, the Middle Ages have often been called the 'Dark Ages'. During this tour, you will find out that they were not. The Middle Ages were an interesting time, and they were full of **scientific** discoveries. During this time, inventions and **technology** from India, China, North Africa, and the Middle East were brought to Europe.

Inventions and machines **designed** by medieval scholars made a great contribution to society, and many are still in use today. And some of these inventions are very common. For example, the first fountain pen was made in 953 in Africa. Before then, people used bird feathers and ink to write with. This method would often leave your fingers and clothes covered with black ink. So the first fountain pen had a small container with ink inside and did not stain people's clothes or fingers while the user was writing. You can see a model of this fountain pen in Room 11B. In the same room, you'll find early examples of eyeglasses. Eyeglasses were **invented** In Italy in the thirteenth century. No one knows who invented them. The first eyeglasses were held in front of the eyes or balanced on the nose. They were **developed** to help people with bad vision

to read. But let's now move on to some other inventions.

In rooms 12A and 12B we have works by the great medieval engineer, Al-Jazari. Al-Jazari lived in twelfth-century Turkey. His work *The Book of Knowledge of Ingenious Mechanical Devices* lists one hundred different machines with instructions and **diagrams** explaining how to build them. In this exhibition, you can see models of some of the **devices** that were designed by al-Jazari. Here, you can see his mechanical clocks. Water and weights make the clocks work. However, his most important invention was the crankshaft. The crankshaft is a long arm that allows machines to move in a straight line. It was first used for watering gardens and fields on farms. In more modern times, a crankshaft is used in car engines.

As we move along, you'll find one of the most important inventions of medieval times. This invention has changed the history of the world in ways that we can't even imagine. It's one of the four great inventions of Chinese culture: gunpowder. Gunpowder was invented in the ninth century by Chinese scientists who were trying to create a powder that would make you live forever. They weren't successful, of course, but their attempts led to the invention of fireworks and weapons. The first instructions on how to make gunpowder were written in the eleventh century by Zeng Gongliang, Ding Du, and Yang Weide. The invention of gunpowder has changed the way we fight wars. It changed the outcome of many medieval battles and affected the history of the world. Many people think gunpowder is the most important invention in history. Now, let's move to the next room, which is all about medieval medicine …

🔊 6.2

1 Inventions and technology from India, China, North Africa, and the Middle East were brought to Europe.

2 The first eyeglasses were held in front of the eyes or balanced on the nose.

3 The crankshaft is a long arm that allows machines to move in a straight line.

4 As we move along, you'll find one of the most important inventions of medieval times.

🔊 6.3

1 The Middle Ages were an interesting time, and they were full of scientific discoveries.

2 Inventions and machines designed by medieval scholars made a great contribution to society, and many are still in use today. And some of these inventions are very common.

3 Many people think gunpowder is the most important invention in history.

🔊 6.4

Good morning! In today's lecture I want to discuss an invention that has changed our lives. This **product** has made a huge difference in the way we work, travel, communicate, and socialize with friends. Can you guess what it is? I'm talking here about cell phone **apps**. The word *app* comes from *application*. Traditionally, applications were used in computers to help them perform better. However, with the invention of smartphones, the word *app* is used to refer to phone applications. In this lecture, we'll start by discussing the very first apps and their development. We will then discuss how apps have changed our lives. Finally, we'll focus on some of the most popular apps used by people today.

🔊 6.5

I'd like to start by talking a little bit about the first apps. These were included with each smartphone. These types of apps were placed in the phones to help **users access** the Internet, check emails, send texts, and so on. The first apps were designed to increase efficiency at work and **allow** people to access important information. However, it was the second generation of apps that really changed things. These were downloadable apps. Users simply downloaded apps from the Internet and **installed** them on their phones. Since its introduction, the app market has grown far beyond anyone's expectations. The first app store was opened in 2008. By 2011, it was

reporting over 10 billion downloads, and people were using apps more than Internet browsers on their phones. And by 2015, an estimated 100 billion apps had been downloaded. These numbers have been growing ever since.

These numbers give us a good idea about how popular apps are and how quickly they've developed. People from all over the world use apps for entertainment, travel, and communication. So, I'm going to briefly talk about how these apps have changed our lives. It's hard to imagine life before smartphones and cell phone apps – or, for those of us who are old enough, to remember it. But let's go ahead and make an attempt anyway. So, imagine for a moment that you're taking a road trip in the days before smartphones. Weeks before the trip, you go to the bookstore or library to get some guidebooks about the places you're going to visit. A few days before you leave, you get some audio books to entertain you during the long trip. You go to the store and buy some maps – yes, the paper kind. The day before the trip, you sit down at your computer and look up the directions and print them out. Then, you pack some of your favorite CDs to bring along. You also pack your camera – and your flashlight, in case your car breaks down. And you write down some phone numbers and addresses – of the friends you'll be visiting and the hotels where you'll be staying.

While you're driving, your passenger reads the directions to you and looks for street signs. If you get lost, you stop at a gas station to ask for directions. You have to write them down on a piece of paper. OK, so I think you get the idea. Now let's make a comparison with the same trip today. No books, no maps, no CDs, no lists of phone numbers, no friend giving you directions – the smartphone does it all! Think of the apps you'd use just for that one trip. You'd read reviews and book your hotel with a travel app. The GPS would replace the directions and maps and your friend in the front seat. Of course, a music app would replace the CDs, and you could listen to podcasts, as well as audio books. And, of course, you wouldn't need to bring a camera or a flashlight. Yes, we've certainly made a lot of progress since the pre-smartphone days!

So, now I'd like to mention another important effect of the invention of apps. It has **created** a whole new IT sector. It is one of the fastest-growing **industries**, and there is a great need for skilled software engineers.

But apps have also had some negative effects. For one thing, people have become more helpless because they're so dependent on their phones for information. For example, if they're in a place with no cell phone signal, they're not very good at asking for and following directions. And apps have made people less patient because they expect to have information immediately. In fact, a recent study found that 50 percent of smartphone users leave a web page if it doesn't load in 10 seconds.

OK, in the next part of the lecture, I'll discuss some of the most common apps in more detail …

🔊 6.6

I would like to present an invention that has made the way we organize our work easier. It's a simple invention, and most of you have used it. It's a small yellow piece of paper that is known all over the world. It's the Post-it® note. A Post-it® note is a piece of paper with special glue on the back. Modern Post-it® notes can be any color or shape. Post-it® notes are simple to use. You can stick them on anything and the note will stay in place. The notes can be easily removed from any surface. First, I am going to talk about the history of this invention. Then, I will explain how it has made a difference in our lives.

🔊 6.7

1: This is a typewriter from the 1950s. As you can see, it has a keyboard like a computer, and the user strikes a key that strikes a sheet of paper.

You move the paper as you type, by pulling the lever on the left.

2: This chart gives information about the number of students who bought ebooks here on campus. According to the college bookstore, in 2010, only about 62 students used ebooks. Two years later, that number doubled to 122. More and more people used ebooks after that. The numbers were up to 324 in 2014 and 540 in 2016.

3: We interviewed fifty people on campus about how often they shop online. This chart shows the results. We can see that twenty-five percent – that's a quarter – said that they buy something online three to four times a week. Fifty-two percent said that they shop online three or four times a month. Nineteen percent shop online three or four times a year. And four percent of the people we interviewed said that they do not shop online at all.

4: This diagram shows the basic functionality of an online quiz. The left side shows the student, and as you can see, the student can log in, take a quiz, and get his or her results. On the right, you can see the functions of the administrator: to log the student out, add a category, and add or edit questions to the quiz.

UNIT 7

▶ The Growth of Louis Vuitton

Narrator: The Louis Vuitton company started in Paris in 1854 making expensive luggage for the rich and famous. In the last 25 years they've branched out into luxury clothing. A coat will cost you up to $5,000 and a handbag as much as $150,000. Here's Dana Thomas, an expert on luxury brands, to explain more about their sales strategy.

Dana Thomas: In 1977, Louis Vuitton only had two stores, and now it's an enormous business.

Narrator: They now have over 400 stores all over the world.

Dana Thomas: It's a delicate balance of selling masses to the masses while still remaining exclusive to the rich. You have a pyramid. At the top you have the very beautifully-made, exclusive, limited amount product. They will make anything you want. From there, you have the middle range that you can walk into the store and you can buy it. It's still very well-made – beautiful fabrics. And then you have the bottom range where the money comes in, where they just sell masses of stuff. It could be a perfume, wallets, belts, scarves, umbrellas, key chains, sunglasses. That's how they manage to keep people like the Sultan of Brunei, Hollywood stars, royalty, as customers, as well as selling to the Chinese secretary who wants to put the bag on her desk to show that she can afford a Louis Vuitton bag.

Narrator: So even if we can't afford the top or the middle of the pyramid, we can at least buy their belts to hold up our pants.

🔊 7.1

Clara: Do you have any ideas for our research project?

Adele: I've been looking for an interesting topic, but to be honest, I haven't come up with anything yet. Can you give me a hand?

Clara: Well, I have been reading about fashion of the future, new **designs**, new technology, and all that.

Adele: Do you mean the kinds of clothes that we're going to be wearing in the future?

Clara: Not really. It's more about future **fabrics** and how we're going to use them.

Adele: Well?

Clara: OK. I've found out that there are designers who create eco-clothes.

Adele: Eco-clothes?

Clara: Yeah. They're clothes that are not only good for the community but also environmentally friendly. The designers make sure that the clothes aren't made by people working in bad conditions. **Local** workshops are set up so that people can earn a good salary. And eco-friendly clothing typically helps protect the environment, too, apparently.

Adele: How do they work, exactly?

Clara: Well, there are fabrics that collect the energy from when you move. Then, the energy is **converted** into electricity.

Adele: Interesting. So, a few years from now, we'll probably be using this fabric to charge our phones, right?

Clara: Well, as long as you keep moving, yes!

Adele: That reminds me of **smart** fabrics. I saw an exhibit about them at the science festival. Some scientists are working on fabrics that can kill bacteria and regulate body temperature.

Clara: Wow! How does that work?

Adele: Well, these fabrics keep your body temperature the same in any kind of weather. And I read that they can be used to make sports clothing, which would help people who exercise in very cold or very hot climates.

Clara: Really? That is amazing.

Adele: I've also read that there are other fabrics that can help reduce muscle aches and prevent us from getting sick.

Clara: Wow, that is so cool. You know, I saw a fashion show once where the designers used lights in the clothes. It was a dress made from lights. They change color as you move.

Adele: But what was the point of that?

Clara: Well, I do agree that it's not very **practical**. I don't think there are many people dying to wear a dress made of lights. It sounds like someone designed it just for the fun of it.

Adele: I'm not crazy about that idea, to be honest. As far as I'm concerned, a dress made from lights is **useless**. Anyway, it looks like we've finally come up with some good ideas.

Clara: Yeah, I agree. So, we have clothes that are environmentally friendly, clothes that help with our health, and clothes that use technology. Which one should we **focus on**?

Adele: I like the idea of clothes that help people with health problems.

Clara: Are you sure? It seems pretty complicated.

Adele: Yeah, I think it'll be fine. I do think it'll be interesting, and there are a lot of different articles on the topic.

Clara: OK, let's do it!

🔊 7.2

1 a I've been reading about fashion of the future.
  b I have been reading about fashion of the future.
2 a That's amazing.
  b That is amazing.
3 a I agree that it's not very practical.
  b I do agree that it's not very practical.
4 a I think it'll be interesting.
  b I do think it'll be interesting.

🔊 7.3

1 I've been looking for an interesting topic, but to be honest, I haven't come up with anything yet.
2 And eco-friendly clothing typically helps protect the environment, too.
3 Well, these fabrics keep your body temperature the same in any kind of weather.
4 Anyway, it looks like we've finally come up with some good ideas.
5 There are a lot of different articles on the topic.

🔊 7.4

Host: In today's show, we'll be interviewing the talented fashion designer Aysha Al-Husaini. Hot on the heels of her fashion week show, Aysha's new **collection** is all the rage in Doha. She turned the heads of the fashion world with her **unique** designs, which **combine** traditional Muslim fashion with French chic. Aysha, thank you for coming to the studio.

Aysha: Thank you for having me.

Host: First of all, can you tell me where you get your ideas from?

Aysha: Well, I come from a Muslim family. My parents are both from Qatar. I was born there, but then we traveled a lot. I went to school in New York and I went to a design school there. These days, I spend my time traveling between Qatar and the United States.

🔊 7.5

Host: How did you feel about growing up in New York?

Aysha: Well, as a teenager in New York, I had a lot of problems trying to dress in a **modest** way. For example, when you look at the summer fashion in New York, the trend is always to wear skirts, shorts, and sleeveless shirts. I didn't feel comfortable wearing them, but at the same time my friends thought it was strange to wear long sleeves and jeans in the summer. So I've always tried to combine my culture with fashion. As a teenager, I would make my own clothes, like colorful skirts and scarves. I wanted my designs to be **individual**. They were unique, and eventually people **admired** my clothes rather than laughed at me.

Host: I see. So, do you know what ideas most people have about Muslim clothes?

Aysha: Well, it's a hot topic at the moment, but I think there's a lot of misunderstanding about Muslim clothes. The thing is that when you say *Muslim fashion*, people in New York think of a *burka*. You know, like the blue or black cloaks that cover women from head to toe.

Host: And could you explain what you think Muslim fashion is?

Aysha: Let me give you an example. When I first started at design school, my teachers would ask me strange questions, such as how I was going to stay in the fashion business if I'm not going to design miniskirts or sleeveless shirts. But as far as I'm concerned, there is much more to fashion than showing your body. There are millions of Muslim women who live in the United States and Europe who want to wear fashionable clothes. There are also women who simply like to dress in a modest way.

Host: So, are you saying that there is a need for fashionable clothes for Muslim women?

Aysha: Absolutely. We want to be fashionable and be ourselves at the same time. My feeling is this: I want to create clothes that are modest, but at the same time, give women **confidence** – clothes that allow women to be themselves.

Host: I see what you mean. So, how would you describe your **style**?

Aysha: Well, many reviewers have described my style as "traditional chic," and I guess I'd agree with them. What I think is that combining traditional with chic is a huge area in fashion. When you look at the work of other designers in China and India, you can see that many traditional styles are being reused by young designers. Above all, people like to be individuals and show their cultural roots – they like to show where they come from.

Host: As I understand it, your designs are must-haves for Muslim women outside the United States as well. Could you tell me more about that?

Aysha: Yes. In addition to New York and Paris, I sell my collection in big cities like Doha, Dubai, and Abu Dhabi. Another thing is that I also receive requests for my clothes from women in Pakistan, Indonesia, Singapore, and Malaysia, so someday I might open stores there.

Host: Thank you for coming to the studio today.

Aysha: It was my pleasure. Anytime!

🔊 7.6

Host: In today's show, we'll be interviewing the talented fashion designer Aysha Al-Husaini. Hot on the heels of her fashion week show, Aysha's new **collection** is all the rage in Doha. She turned the heads of the fashion world with her **unique** designs, which **combine** traditional Muslim fashion with French chic. Aysha, thank you for coming to the studio.

Aysha: Thank you for having me.

Host: First of all, can you tell me where you get your ideas from?

Aysha: Well, I come from a Muslim family. My parents are both from Qatar. I was born there, but then we traveled a lot. I went to school in New York and I went to a design school there. These days, I spend my time traveling between Qatar and the United States.

Host: How did you feel about growing up in New York?

Aysha: Well, as a teenager in New York, I had a lot of problems trying to dress in a **modest** way. For example, when you look at the summer fashion in New York, the trend is always to wear skirts, shorts, and sleeveless shirts. I didn't feel comfortable wearing them, but at the same time my friends thought it was strange to wear long sleeves and jeans in the summer. So I've always tried to combine my culture with fashion. As a teenager, I would make my own clothes, like colorful skirts and scarves. I wanted my designs to be **individual**. They were unique, and eventually people **admired** my clothes rather than laughed at me.

Host: I see. So, do you know what ideas most people have about Muslim clothes?

Aysha: Well, it's a hot topic at the moment, but I think there's a lot of misunderstanding about Muslim clothes. The thing is that when you say *Muslim fashion*, people in New York think of a *burka*. You know, like the blue or black cloaks that cover women from head to toe.

Host: And could you explain what you think Muslim fashion is?

Aysha: Let me give you an example. When I first started at design school, my teachers would ask me strange questions, such as how I was going to stay in the fashion business if I'm not going to design miniskirts or sleeveless shirts. But as far as I'm concerned, there is much more to fashion than showing your body. There are millions of Muslim women who live in the United States and Europe who want to wear fashionable clothes. There are also women who simply like to dress in a modest way.

Host: So, are you saying that there is a need for fashionable clothes for Muslim women?

Aysha: Absolutely. We want to be fashionable and be ourselves at the same time. My feeling is this: I want to create clothes that are modest, but at the same time, give women **confidence** – clothes that allow women to be themselves.

Host: I see what you mean. So, how would you describe your **style**?

Aysha: Well, many reviewers have described my style as "traditional chic," and I guess I'd agree with them. What I think is that combining traditional with chic is a huge area in fashion. When you look at the work of other designers in China and India, you can see that many traditional styles are being reused by young designers. Above all, people like to be individuals and show their cultural roots – they like to show where they come from.

Host: As I understand it, your designs are must-haves for Muslim women outside the United States as well. Could you tell me more about that?

Aysha: Yes. In addition to New York and Paris, I sell my collection in big cities like Doha, Dubai, and Abu Dhabi. Another thing is that I also receive requests for my clothes from women in Pakistan, Indonesia, Singapore, and Malaysia, so someday I might open stores there.

Host: Thank you for coming to the studio today.

Aysha: It was my pleasure. Anytime!

🔊 7.7

Clara: OK ... So, we're going to do the research project on fabrics that help people with health problems. Did you say you already found some articles, Adele?

Adele: Yes. I can send you the links tonight.

Clara: Great! Thank you!

Adele: But we'll need to make a presentation. How will we know what to include?

Clara: Hmm. Well, maybe we should just get some ideas first. How long does the presentation have to be?

Adele: Fifteen minutes. And we have to have an outline by next Wednesday.

Clara: Oh! Wow. OK ...

Adele: Well, how about I send you the links, and then we both look at the articles and take some notes ... and we meet up again on Monday? What do you think?

Clara: OK. Then, on Monday we can plan the outline.

Adele: That sounds good. Will we need to use presentation software?

Clara: Yes, I think so. But maybe we should work on the outline first. Then, next week we can work on the presentation.

Adele: I haven't done a presentation before. Can we use the computer in the classroom? Or should we bring a laptop to class?

Clara: Oh ... good question. I can bring my laptop. But we should probably check if that's OK.

Adele: We could ask on Wednesday in class.

Clara: Good idea. Let's check with the professor on Wednesday.

Adele: OK, so we'll do some research this weekend. Then, we'll meet again on Monday to make an outline.

Clara: Sounds like a plan.

Adele: OK. Great.

Clara: See you then!

UNIT 8

▶ **Workshops for Entrepreneurs**

Reporter: When Marie LaQuerre got laid off, she had an idea to make and sell a line of children's novelties.

Marie LaQuerre: My company name is actually Goobity Goo.

Reporter: What she didn't have was thousands of dollars to buy a laser cutter to create her products.

Marie LaQuerre: That machine can do, like, everything, it seems like.

Reporter: The day the iPad was announced, Patrick Buckley had an idea for a custom-made cover. What he didn't have was the expensive, computerized woodcutting machine he needed to produce a prototype. LaQuerre, Buckley, and scores of other budding entrepreneurs have become members of TechShop in Menlo Park, California, a place for do-it-yourselfers, inventors, and dreamers.

Mark Hatch: We believe that every kitchen should come with compressed air, electricity, and a vise.

Reporter: Mark Hatch is TechShop's CEO.

Mark Hatch: Most don't. You know, people get to come here and use ours.

Reporter: Here's the drill. Joining TechShop is a little like joining a health club, except here, for $100 a month, instead of running on a treadmill, you get to run industrial-strength machinery.

Members have access to the latest in computer-assisted design and machine tools that would cost a fortune to buy.

Mark Hatch: We teach people in an afternoon how to make things. We have a lot of entrepreneurs.

Reporter: With the tools at TechShop, Phil Hughes developed a way to cool computer servers that could save vast amounts of energy.

Phil Hughes: This pulls at it. All the heat is at the server, from the server to the lid.

Reporter: For now, his company, Clustered Systems, has its world headquarters at TechShop. But a partnership with Emerson, the huge appliance manufacturer, could change that.

Phil Hughes: They expect to sell thousands and thousands of these things, which is going to make us very happy.

Reporter: And perhaps very rich?

Phil Hughes: Well, yes. Why not?

Reporter: For $100 a month another member is building a lunar landing module for an XPrize competition.

Man: Where else can I find someplace that I can store my lunar lander?

Reporter: Marie LaQuerre is now selling her products online and in a few retail stores. Patrick Buckley's iPad cover is taking off, and 30 people have been hired to make it.

Patrick Buckley: We're on track to do between $3 and $5 million this year.

Reporter: And TechShop is doing well too, expanding to eight more locations. Evidence that in America today, money may be tight, but ideas and ambition are flowing freely.

🔊 8.1

In this week's program, I'd like to talk about a book that has changed the way I think about money. It's called *The Secret of Being Wealthy*. It was written by a business school graduate named John Holm who decided to study the behavior of wealthy people. He paid close attention to what rich people do: checking where they eat, what they buy, how they live, and so on. The results of his study were pretty surprising.

🔊 8.2

When you think of someone who is very rich, what comes to mind? Most people think that rich people live lavish lifestyles — that is, they drive very expensive cars, eat in expensive restaurants, own a yacht, or live in big houses. But, as John Holm discovered, people who have money don't actually do these things. Most **millionaires** actually seem to have ordinary lifestyles. In other words, they have normal cars, average houses, and so on. On the other hand, people who *look* rich — the people who drive the latest Ferrari or only wear designer clothes — may not actually be rich at all. Instead, they have spent all their money trying to show off — showing other people that they might be wealthy. In other words, having expensive things is not always a sign that someone is rich.

So, what do millionaires do, and what can we learn from them? Well, millionaires are often financially savvy. To put it another way, they're smart about how to save and spend money. The first important thing is that millionaires always have a good handle on their budget. In other words, they know how much they're spending. According to Holm, around 75 percent of millionaires know exactly how much money they have, and they know exactly how much they spend on food, bills, clothes, etc. As a result, they don't spend too much, and they don't get into **debt**. They can plan for the future and save their money. To sum up, the lesson here is that you should never spend more money than you have!

Another surprising fact is that millionaires usually have simple lifestyles. They have nice houses and nice cars, but they don't spend all their money on these things. In fact, most rich people stay in the same place for a very long time and don't live in big, expensive palaces. Indeed, according to John Holm, half of millionaires have lived in the same house for 20 years. Also, around 65 percent of millionaires live in homes that cost $350,000 or less. Again, the important lesson here is to live within your means – that is, don't spend more money than you have. If you spend all your **savings** on a luxury BMW, then you probably aren't rich – you just want to look rich. In fact, the study reveals that 86 percent of luxury cars are bought by people who can't **afford** them. Most rich people don't have bank **loans** – they only spend a small percentage of what they have, and they save or invest the rest.

Now here is an interesting fact. The study shows that most millionaires have very happy relationships. Not only are they married, but they stay married for a long time. In John Holm's opinion, this is very important because of the golden rule about **saving money**. There is no doubt that it's more difficult to save money if you are single. One effect of being a couple is that it's easier to save money. If there are two of you, it's easier to pay attention to what money you have and what you're spending.

And of course, people who don't have huge bank loans and debts are happier. If you don't have to worry about the monthly credit card **payments**, you're less likely to buy things to make you feel better. People with debt often spend more time shopping, just to make themselves feel happier, but real millionaires don't need to do this.

So, what can we learn from the wealthy? The answer is surprisingly simple. Don't spend more money than you have. Don't get into debt or take out bank loans. Pay close attention to your money, and don't spend time trying to show other people that you're rich. In John Holm's opinion, being "wealthy" is a feeling. That is, it doesn't mean being rich or having millions of dollars. It means being happy with what you have.

🔊 **8.3**

1 Most people think that rich people live lavish lifestyles, that is they drive very expensive cars, eat in expensive restaurants, own a yacht, or live in big houses.

2 In other words, having expensive things is not always a sign that someone is rich.

3 On the other hand, people who look rich – the people who drive the latest Ferrari or only wear designer clothes – may not actually be rich at all.

4 As a result, they don't spend too much, and they don't get into debt.

5 There is no doubt that it's more difficult to save money if you are single.

6 So, what can we learn from the wealthy? The answer is surprisingly simple.

🔊 **8.4**

Host: In today's program, we discuss the recent **decision** made by several colleges to give students money in return for good grades. Students will be paid by the hour to take additional math and science classes. The students who improve their grades and keep their grade average high will be given cash rewards at the end of each semester. To discuss this new project, we have invited education expert Dr. Michael Burns, and we welcome your calls during the program. We'd like to hear your opinion: Do you think college students should be paid for good grades?

🔊 **8.5**

Host: Dr. Burns, thank you for coming today. Can you tell us more about the project? Where does this idea come from?

Dr. Burns: Thank you. Well, the idea of paying students for their work isn't new. For example, in some high schools in New York City and Memphis, Tennessee, students are paid $40 a month for good attendance and are paid extra for good grades. They also get $50 for taking a college entrance exam. The goal of these programs is to **encourage** students to finish their education and be able to get a good job in the future. Many students who fail or drop out do so because they come from low-income families. They might have to work after school and on the weekends to help support the family. Because of that, they often have no time to study. We want to make sure that all students have the same opportunities in their future.

Host: I see. Let's hear from our first caller. Mariam Hassan is the president of a medium-sized university. Dr. Hassan?

Dr. Hassan: Hello. Yes, I recently read about this new program, and I really don't think it's a good idea. I understand that many students drop out of college because of financial problems. At my college alone, the dropout rate is over 25 percent. However, will paying students really encourage them to continue? In my experience, it won't. Of course, the statistics are terrible, but I'm not confident that this program will solve the real problems – it may just cover them up. I think the money would be better spent on student **services**, like hiring additional professors and advisors. Two of the reasons why students drop out are stress and poor time management. Advisors can help students learn to **manage** their time better. As a consequence, students will do better in school and will be more likely to graduate.

Dr. Burns: I can see your point, but we have already spent a lot on student services. I think that paying students to study will show them that we treat them like adults. It will give them a **sense** of responsibility. College students are young adults, and so when they have a choice between staying in college and studying or going to work and making money, they often make the wrong choice. They want to have money so that they can buy things for themselves. Besides, we don't want to pay them a lot. I think we're simply giving them an option: stay in school and be paid, or get a **minimum wage** job.

Host: Christine Thorne is a parent with two children in college.

Mrs. Thorne: Hello. I was very worried when I heard about this new program. I realize that students need encouragement to stay in school, but are we going in the right direction? First of all, I feel that we're sending the students the wrong message. Learning should be about studying new things and being **responsible**. Personally, I think the students who aren't interested in studying will simply take the easy courses to keep their average grade high and get the cash. I believe that we should focus more on rewarding excellent schools and teachers, and not on students who might be lazy.

Dr. Burns: These are all good points, but I don't think that this view applies to all students. Not all parents are educated or interested in studying. They pass this bad attitude on to their own children. Then the children don't see the benefits of learning. To change this image, we need to show them a good reason for studying.

Host: Thank you. Let's have a look now at some of the comments we've received during the program.

🔊 8.6

Host: Dr. Burns, thank you for coming today. Can you tell us more about the project? Where does this idea come from?

Dr. Burns: Thank you. Well, the idea of paying students for their work isn't new. For example, in some high schools in New York City and Memphis, Tennessee, students are paid $40 a month for good attendance and are paid extra for good grades. They also get $50 for taking a college entrance exam. The goal of these programs is to encourage students to finish their education and be able to get a good job in the future. Many students who fail or drop out do so because they come from low-income families. They might have to work after school and on the weekends to help support the family. Because of that, they often have no time to study. We want to make sure that all students have the same opportunities in their future.

Host: I see. Let's hear from our first caller. Mariam Hassan is the president of a medium-sized university. Dr. Hassan?

Dr. Hassan: Hello. Yes, I recently read about this new program, and I really don't think it's a good idea. I understand that many students drop out of college because of financial problems. At my college alone, the dropout rate is over 25 percent. However, will paying students really encourage them to continue? In my experience, it won't. Of course, the statistics are terrible, but I'm not confident that this program will solve the real problems – it may just cover them up. I think the money would be better spent on student services, like hiring additional professors and advisors. Two of the reasons why students drop out are stress and poor time management. Advisors can help students learn to manage their time better. As a consequence, students will do better in school and will be more likely to graduate.

🔊 8.7

Advisor: Hello, Daniel. It's nice to meet you.

Daniel: Nice to meet you.

Advisor: First of all, welcome to college! I'm your academic advisor, and I'm going to help you figure out which classes to take.

Daniel: Thank you.

Advisor: Now ... I see you're interested in economics?

Daniel: I think so, but I'm not really sure. When do I have to declare my major?

Advisor: Not yet. Not until the end of your second year.

Daniel: That's good. But can I take some economics classes before that?

Advisor: Oh yes. You can and you should! You can take Introduction to Economics ... probably next semester. You have to take calculus first. It's a prerequisite.

Daniel: So should I take the calculus class this semester?

Advisor: Yes ... um ... you should also take computer science. Both of those are prerequisites.

Daniel: OK.

Advisor: Those two classes will count for seven credits.

Daniel: How many credits should I take altogether?

Advisor: Most students take between 12 and 16. Don't take too many classes for your first semester. You need time to get used to college.

Daniel: Do I need to take general education credits?

Advisor: Yes. The university requires at least 15 general education credits. There's a lot of choice. You could take history, music, public speaking ... even physical education or dance.

Daniel: Could I take a class in art history?

Advisor: Of course!

Daniel: I'd like to do that. I'm very interested in art.

Advisor: Then that's a good choice. So ... probably one more class will be enough. That should be Writing 101.

Daniel: Writing? Really?

Advisor: Yes. You have to take several writing classes. We expect our graduates to be able to read and write well.

Daniel: OK.

Advisor: So that's four classes: calculus, computer science, art history and, uh, Writing 101.

Daniel: How do I register for classes?

Advisor: You can do that online. You should register before Friday. But first, let's work out a schedule that works for you. Now, on Mondays ...

CREDITS

The authors and publishers acknowledge the following sources of copyright material and are grateful for the permissions granted. While every effort has been made, it has not always been possible to identify the sources of all the material used, or to trace all copyright holders. If any omissions are brought to our notice, we will be happy to include the appropriate acknowledgements on reprinting and in the next update to the digital edition, as applicable.

Photo credits:

Key: T = Top, C = Center, B = Below, L = Left, R = Right.

p. 12: Cultura RM Exclusive/Peter Muller/Getty Images; pp. 14–15: Thinkstock/Getty Images; p. 20: Peter Charlesworth/LightRocket/Getty Images; p. 21: jpbcpa/E+/Getty Images; p. 26 (L): Daniel J Cox/Oxford Scientific/Getty Images; p. 26 (C): Olaf Kruger/Getty Images; p. 26 (R): Andy Rouse/The Image Bank/Getty Images; pp. 36–37: Bloomberg/Getty Images; p. 41: Yoshikazu Tsuno/AFP/Getty Images; p. 42: The Asahi Shimbun/Getty Images; p. 46: Aris Messinis/AFP/Getty Images; p. 47: Peteri/Shutterstock; p. 56: asiseeit/E+/Getty Images; pp. 58–59: Medioimages/Photodisc/Getty Images; p. 63: Jeff Greenberg/Photolibrary/Getty Images; p. 66 (syringe): Peter Dazeley/Photographer's Choice/Getty Images; p. 66 (spider): specnaz-s/iStock/Getty Images; p. 69: Roberto Machado Noa/LightRocket/Getty Images; p. 70: Panoramic Images/Getty Images; p. 72: Roberto Westbrook/Blend Images/Getty Images; p. 76: Jordan Siemens/Iconica/Getty Images; p. 78, p. 166: Sam Edwards/OJO Images/Getty Images; pp. 80–81: Suttipong Sutiratanachai/Moment/Getty Images; p. 86: Hero Images/Getty Images; pp. 102–103: frans lemmens/Alamy; p. 106 (photo a): Inti St Clair/Blend Images/Getty Images; p. 106 (photo b), p. 107 (photo d): Image Source/Getty Images; p. 107 (photo c): Image Source RF/Raphye Alexius/Getty Images; p. 108: AFP/Getty Images; p. 114 (meditation): Betsie Van der Meer/Iconica/Getty Images; p. 114 (soccer): Thomas Barwick/Taxi/Getty Images; p. 114 (biking), p. 144 (C): Westend61/Getty Images; p. 114 (acupuncture): Bridget Borsheim/Stockbyte/Getty Images; p. 123 (T): Hemant Mehta/Canopy/Getty Images; p. 123 (C): pixdeluxe/E+/Getty Images; pp. 124–125: Vidler Steve/Prisma/age fotostock; p. 129 (photo a): Dorling Kindersley/Getty Images; p. 129 (photo b): Sergey Goruppa/Shutterstock; p. 129 (photo c): DEA/A. DAGLI ORTI/De Agostini/Getty Images; p. 129 (photo d): Nataliya Hora/Shutterstock; p. 132 (L): Triff/Shutterstock; p. 132 (C): Tischenko Irina/Shutterstock; p. 132 (R): View Stock/Getty Images; p. 135: ahmetemre/iStock/Getty Images; p. 139 (credit card): pagadesign/E+/Getty Images; p. 139 (microwave): scanrail/iStock/Getty Images; p. 139 (refrigerator): 3alexd/E+/Getty Images; p. 139 (car): Rawpixel Ltd/E+/Getty Images; p. 141: Vitaly Korovin/Shutterstock; pp. 146–147: Samir Hussein/WireImages/Getty Images; p. 150 (L): Steve Russell/Toronto Star/Getty Images; p. 150 (R): Chung Sung-Jun/Getty Images News/Getty Images; p. 157: Pete Saloutos/Image Source/Getty Images; p. 164: Cultura Exclusive/DUEL/Getty Images; pp. 168–169: Digital Vision/Photodisc/Getty Images; p. 173: DeltaOFF/iStock/Getty Images; pp. 174–175: Paul Williams - Funkystock/imageBROKER/Getty Images; p. 176: Lane Oatey/Getty Images; p. 186: Image Source/InStock/Image Source/Getty Images.

Front cover photographs by (woman) Amazingmikael/Shutterstock and (park) romakoma/Shutterstock.

Illustrations

by Clive Goodyer (Beehive): p. 24; Fiona Gowen: p. 41; Ben Hasler (NB Illustration) p. 85 (A–D, F); Oxford Designers & Illustrators: p. 85 (E).

Video Stills Supplied by BBC Worldwide Learning.

Video Supplied by BBC Worldwide Learning.

Corpus

Development of this publication has made use of the Cambridge English Corpus (CEC). The CEC is a multi-billion word computer database of contemporary spoken and written English. It includes British English, American English, and other varieties of English. It also includes the Cambridge Learner Corpus, developed in collaboration with the University of Cambridge ESOL Examinations. Cambridge University Press has built up the CEC to provide evidence about language use that helps to produce better language teaching materials

Cambridge Dictionaries

Cambridge dictionaries are the world's most widely used dictionaries for learners of English. The dictionaries are available in print and online at dictionary.cambridge.org. Copyright © Cambridge University Press, reproduced with permission.

Typeset by emc design ltd

Audio production by CityVox New York

INFORMED BY TEACHERS

Classroom teachers shaped everything about *Prism*. The topics. The exercises. The critical thinking skills. The On Campus sections. Everything. We are confident that *Prism* will help your students succeed in college because teachers just like you helped guide the creation of this series.

Prism Advisory Panel

The members of the *Prism* Advisory Panel provided inspiration, ideas, and feedback on many aspects of the series. *Prism* is stronger because of their contributions.

Gloria Munson
University of Texas, Arlington

Kim Oliver
Austin Community College

Gregory Wayne
Portland State University

Julaine Rosner
Mission College

Dinorah Sapp
University of Mississippi

Christine Hagan
George Brown College/Seneca College

Heidi Lieb
Bergen Community College

Stephanie Kasuboski
Cuyahoga Community College

Global Input

Teachers from more than 500 institutions all over the world provided valuable input through:

- Surveys
- Focus Groups
- Reviews